This is my book.

My name is:

Karli Howard

from Mr. & Mrs. Wilkinson

**This book will
help me learn
more about God!**

Getting the Big Picture

Are you ready for something big? The whole Bible gives you a big picture of what God is like. God wants you to know the big picture about Him. He loves you very much. He wants you to spend time with Him every day. That will help you know Him better.

This time with God is called a "quiet time." You can think about God. You can read about God. You can talk to Him in prayer.

This book will help you with your quiet time. You will get the big picture about God. You will find out what He says in the Bible.

Choose a time to spend with God each day. It may be when you first get up. It may be just before you go to bed. There is a new story in this book for every day. After you read all the stories, go back and read them again!

This book is special. It has 100 Bible stories just for you! It is written so you can read it yourself. The pictures were drawn by children like you.

Are you ready to start? Every day you can learn more of God's big picture. Here is what to do. You can start with story number one.

- **Talk to God.** Ask Him to help you learn about Him.

- **Read the story.** Each story is from God's Word. You can find it in your own Bible. Read the story carefully. Think about what it says. The stories will help you know how to live God's way.

- **Talk to God again.** The part called "You can pray" will help you get started.

- **Read "God's Word Says."** These words come right from God. They are written for you in the Bible. They will help you understand the story.

- **Read the "Let's Talk" questions.** Think about the answers. You can tell the answers to someone in your family if you want to.

Have fun learning more about God every day!

1. The Beginning

 Have you ever wondered how the world started? How did the sun get in the sky? Where did the animals come from? The Bible tells you. It is called God's Word.

God has always lived. He created the heavens and Earth. God is most powerful of all! He made the heavens and the Earth from nothing! God made light so it would not always be dark. He made the sky.

God moved the water around and made dry land. He made all kinds of plants and trees on the land. They had seeds so more plants could grow. God made the sun, moon and stars. They give the Earth light.

 Next God made all the fish and animals that live in water. He made birds to fly over the Earth. Then God made the animals that live on land. God blessed the things He made so more birds and animals could be born. God saw that everything He had made was good!

God is amazing! He is greater than all His creation. Praise God for His greatness. Thank Him for all He has made!

You Can Pray:
Dear God, You are wonderful! Thank You for the beautiful world You have made! (Tell God about the things He has made that you like best.) In Jesus' name. Amen.

Kylie Kadey   Age 7   Washington

Let's Talk:

1. Who has made the world and everything in it?
2. What is your favorite thing that God has made?
3. Why do you think you should thank God for the world He has made?

2. Creation Completed

 God created the world. He made all the plants and animals. Was that all He created? No! What do you think God made next?

God's most special creation was people! God made a man named Adam. God saw that Adam needed a helper. He made Eve to be Adam's wife. The man and woman were made in the likeness of God. They could know God in ways the animals could not. They could choose right or wrong. They could choose to love God.

People today can still love God. God loves you very much! He wants you to love Him too. The Bible says to love God with all your heart. Pray and tell God you love Him. Choosing to obey God shows you love Him.

God's Word Says:
"Love the LORD your God with all your heart. . . ."
Deuteronomy 6:5

God put Adam and Eve in charge of all the birds and animals. He gave them plants and fruit to eat. God saw that everything He made was very good!

It took God only six days to create everything in the world! On day seven God was done with His work. He took that day to rest.

 You Can Pray:
Dear God, thank You for making me so I can know and love You. (Tell God how you will show you love Him.) In Jesus' name. Amen.

Elena Jordanovska   Age 6   Republic of Macedonia

Let's Talk:

1. What was the last thing God created?
2. What does Deuteronomy 6:5 say God wants you to do?
3. How can you let God know that you love Him?

3. In the Garden

Where do you think is the best place to live? Do you like trees? Would you want to live by a lake? God had a perfect place for Adam and Eve to live!

God made a beautiful garden. It had all kinds of trees. There was fruit to eat. A river watered the garden. Everything was perfect! Adam and Eve lived in this lovely home.

God loved Adam and Eve very much. They loved God too. God walked in the garden and talked to them. It must have been wonderful to talk to God!

God's Word Says:
"Be joyful always; pray continually."
1 Thessalonians 5:16-17

You do not live in the Garden of Eden but you can talk to God. Talking to God is called prayer. Tell God how great He is. Thank God for all He has given you. Tell God about all the things in your life. Talk to Him about other people. God loves it when you talk to Him.

God liked to talk to Adam and Eve too. He told them they could eat the fruit from all the trees in the garden except one. You can find out about that tomorrow.

You Can Pray:
Dear God, thank You for letting me talk to You. Help me remember to tell You about all that happens in my life. In Jesus' name. Amen.

Neema Elias   Age 10   Kenya

Let's Talk:

1. What is your favorite thing about the Garden of Eden?
2. What could Adam and Eve do in the garden?
3. What are some things you will talk to God about?

4. Sin Enters the World

 What kinds of choices do you make every day? You decide to do right or wrong. Adam and Eve had to make choices too.

God said they could eat from any tree in the garden but one. If they ate that fruit, they would be punished. Satan is God's enemy. He lied to Eve about what God had said. She ate the fruit. She gave some to Adam. They disobeyed God.

That was the first sin. Sin is doing what God says is wrong. God must punish sin. Many bad things happened. Adam and Eve had to leave the garden. Some day their bodies would die.

God's Word Says:
" . . . Christ [Jesus] died for our sins. . . ."
1 Corinthians 15:3

 Everyone since then has sinned. You have sinned. God promised to send someone to save people from sin. After many years God sent His perfect Son to Earth. His name was Jesus. He never sinned. Jesus was nailed to a cross. He died for your sin. He was punished for you. Then He came back to life.

Because Jesus died, you can be forgiven. You can trust that Jesus has taken your punishment. You will be saved from sin.

You Can Pray:
Dear God, thank You for sending Jesus to die for my sins. Thank You that I can believe in Jesus. Thank You that my sins can be forgiven. In Jesus' name. Amen.

Jorge Jarquin   Nicaragua

Let's Talk:

1. What did Adam and Eve do that God said was wrong?

2. What is something you have chosen to do wrong?

3. What has Jesus done so your sin can be forgiven?

5. Cain and Abel

 Does God know you love Him? God wants you to have a right attitude toward Him. One brother in this story had a right attitude.

Cain and Abel were sons of Adam and Eve. Abel took care of animals. Cain grew things to eat. Both brothers brought things to give God. Cain brought things he had grown. That was not what God said to do. Abel brought animals from his flock. He obeyed God.

God was happy with Abel and his gift. God knew Abel wanted to please Him. God was not happy with Cain. Cain did not show love for God.

God's Word Says:
" . . . worship in spirit and in truth."
John 4:24

 Cain was very angry that God was not happy with him. Cain was so angry that he killed his brother!

God had to punish Cain. Cain could not be close to God anymore. Crops would not grow for him. He had to move to another land.

God wants you to love Him like Abel did. Do not just pretend. The Bible says to worship God in truth. Be right on the inside when you spend time with God.

 You Can Pray:
Dear God, help me not to pretend. Help me love You more each day. (Tell God about your wrong attitudes you want Him to change.) In Jesus' name. Amen.

Kelsey Hume   Age 7   Missouri

Let's Talk:

1. What gifts did Cain and Abel bring to God?
2. Why did God have to punish Cain?
3. What should your attitude be like when you come to God?

6. A World of Sin

What are some bad things people do today? People hate, kill and steal. In Noah's time the world was full of sin too.

Adam and Eve sinned. They did not obey God. Many more people were born. They were all born wanting to sin. They did terrible things. Everything they thought or did was bad. The world was full of sin.

The sin made God sad. He was sorry He had put people on Earth! God hates sin. He is perfect and holy. He never does anything wrong.

God's Word Says:
"For all have sinned. . . ."
Romans 3:23

God knew He could not ignore sin. He planned to destroy the whole Earth. All the people and animals would die. Sin would be punished.

One man on Earth still loved God. Noah was the only one who chose to do right. God told Noah His plan to destroy the world.

God still has to punish sin. He has not changed. The Bible says everyone has sinned. The wrong things you do are sin. Be glad that Jesus died on the cross and came alive again. He took your punishment.

You Can Pray:
Dear God, thank You for being perfect. Thank You for loving me and sending Jesus to die for me. Help me choose to do right. In Jesus' name. Amen.

Jonathan Olsen   Age 10   Missouri

Let's Talk:
1. How did God feel about the sin in the world?
2. Why does God need to punish sin?
3. Who does the Bible say has sinned?

7. Noah Builds an Ark

God told Noah He was going to destroy the Earth. Everything would die. How would you feel if God told you that? What would you do?

God told Noah what to do. God said to build a huge boat called an ark. He told Noah just how to do it. The ark would be longer than a football field! It would be much taller than a house. God told Noah what kind of wood to use. He told him where to put the door.

God's Word Says:
"This is love for God: to obey his commands. . . ."
1 John 5:3

God was going to send a great flood. Water would cover the whole Earth. Everything would die. God promised to keep Noah and his family safe. They would stay in the ark during the flood.

Every kind of bird and animal came to the ark. Noah needed to take food for his family and all the animals. What a big job! Noah obeyed God. He did everything God told him to do.

God tells you what to do in the Bible. It tells you how to please God. Will you obey what God says in His Word?

You Can Pray:
Dear God, thank You for telling me in the Bible what You want me to do. Help me to obey You today. In Jesus' name. Amen.

Joshua J. Lehman   Age 5   Ohio

Let's Talk:

1. Why did God want Noah to build an ark?
2. What was Noah told to take into the ark?
3. What is one way you can obey God?

8. The Flood

Would you be afraid of the flood that was coming? Noah did not have to be afraid. God had promised to protect him.

Noah was finished with the ark. God told him to take his family inside. That was the only way they could be saved. All the right animals came to Noah. They went into the ark too. Then God closed the door.

Rain fell for 40 days and nights! Water was over the whole world. All the other people and animals on Earth died.

The ark floated on the water. Only Noah and those in the ark with him were still alive. God kept His promise. He saved Noah and his family.

Jesus is the only way you can be saved from your sin. He died on the cross for you. Jesus did not do anything wrong. He took your punishment for sin. After three days God brought Him back to life.

You can choose to believe in Jesus today. Your sin will be forgiven. If you want to believe in Jesus, you can use the prayer below to tell God about it.

You Can Pray:
Dear God, I am sorry I have sinned. I believe Jesus died for my sins and came back to life. Please forgive me and save me. In Jesus' name. Amen.

Mabekar Awuah   Age 10   Ghana

Let's Talk:
1. How long did the rain fall?
2. How did God keep Noah and his family safe in the flood?
3. How can you be saved from your sin?

9. Safe on Dry Land

Do you like to stay in the same place all the time? Noah and his family had been in the ark for many months! They were ready to get back on land.

It took a long time for the water to dry up. At last the Earth was dry. God told Noah to bring his family out of the ark. All the animals came out too. It must have felt good to be on dry land again!

Noah knew that only God had saved his family. Noah thanked God for taking care of them.

You should thank God for taking care of you too. He is with you during good times and bad times. He is with you no matter what happens. The Bible says to give thanks to God. It pleases Him when you thank Him for His care.

God was pleased with Noah's gift. He made a new promise. God would never destroy the whole Earth with a flood again. God put a rainbow in the sky. It reminds God of His promise. A rainbow can remind you of God's care for you.

You Can Pray:
Dear God, thank You so much for taking care of me. (Tell God about some of the ways you know He takes care of you.) In Jesus' name. Amen.

Tamara Wiens   Age 8   Alberta, Canada

Let's Talk:

1. How did Noah know when to get out of the ark?
2. What did Noah do to thank God for taking care of his family?
3. What are some ways God has taken care of you?

10. Time to Move

Have you ever moved to a new place? It can be scary. A long time after the flood a man named Abram had to make a big move.

Abram and his family had lived in the same place for a long time. One day God told Abram to move. God wanted Abram to leave his home. He had to leave the people he knew. He was going to live in a new country.

It would be hard to leave everything he was used to! Abram did not even know where God wanted him to move. God promised to make Abram's family grow. They would be a great new nation.

God's Word Says:
" . . . in God I trust; I will not be afraid. . . ."
Psalm 56:4

Abram trusted God. He did what God asked him to do. Abram and his wife Sarai packed all their things. They took their nephew Lot with them. They left home as God had asked.

There may be times when God asks you to do hard things. Maybe your family has to move. It may be something else. You can trust God like Abram did. He will help you and show you what to do.

You Can Pray:
Dear God, thank You that You know what is best for me. Help me trust You. Help me do the things You ask me to do. In Jesus' name. Amen.

This Bible story can be found in Genesis 12:1-9.

Kayla Olsen   Age 7   Missouri

Let's Talk:

1. What did God want Abram to do?
2. How did Abram show that he trusted God?
3. How can you show that you trust God?

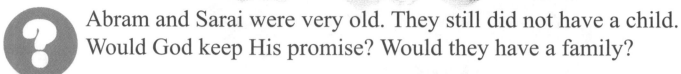

Abram and Sarai were very old. They still did not have a child. Would God keep His promise? Would they have a family?

Abram was 99 years old. God had promised to give him a great family. They would be God's people. God gave Abram and Sarai new names—Abraham and Sarah.

One day three men came to see them. They were God's helpers. Abraham asked them to stay. Sarah made food for them to eat.

God's Word Says:
"I am the LORD, the God of all mankind. Is anything too hard for me?"
Jeremiah 32:27

One of the men gave Abraham good news from God. Sarah would have a baby boy! He would be born the next year. Abraham and Sarah were very old! Sarah laughed. She did not think she could have a baby.

The man wanted Abraham and Sarah to believe God. He said, "Is anything too hard for the LORD?"

God gives you many promises in the Bible. He says He loves you. He says He will help you. Nothing is too hard for God to do. His promises are true. You can always trust God!

Abraham and Sarah would have to wait and see how God would keep His promise.

You Can Pray:
Dear God, I am so happy that You keep Your promises. Thank You! I know I can trust You to do everything You say. In Jesus' name. Amen.

Ashley Shannon   Age 10   Missouri

Let's Talk:

1. What did the men tell Abraham?
2. Why did Sarah laugh when they said she would have a baby?
3. What is one promise from God to you?

12. A Promise Kept

? Is it hard to wait for things? Abraham and Sarah waited a long time. God told them they would have a child. Now it was going to happen!

Sarah was going to have a baby. It would be a little boy. God had promised that. He always keeps His promises.

God's Word Says:
" . . . let us be thankful, and so worship God. . . ."
Hebrews 12:28

The baby was born just as God said. Sarah was so happy! She laughed. God had kept His promise! He had given Abraham and Sarah a son. They named the little boy Isaac. Isaac means "laughter."

People must have been surprised. Abraham was 100 years old! Only God could give Abraham and Sarah a baby when they were old.

Abraham wanted to please God. He did all the things God said to do. He and Sarah thanked God for their new baby.

Have you thanked God? He does many things for you. God helps you every day. He gives you air to breathe. He gives you people to love. God is your helper. Remember to thank Him all the time. God is very good to you!

You Can Pray:
Dear God, You do so much for me! (Thank God for some of the things He does for you.) Help me remember to thank You for all You do. In Jesus' name. Amen.

Makenzie Pulver   Age 6   New York

Let's Talk:

1. Why was Sarah so happy?
2. What did Abraham and Sarah thank God for?
3. Name three things that you can thank God for.

13. A Wife for Isaac

? Has there been a time when you did not know what you should do? You needed help. Find out how God helps a servant in this story.

Isaac was a man now. Abraham wanted him to have a good wife. Abraham sent his servant to find a wife for Isaac.

The servant asked God to show him the right girl. She should give him a drink of water. She should get water for his camels too.

God's Word Says:
"I will . . . teach you in the way you should go. . . ."
Psalm 32:8

Rebekah came to the well. She gave the servant water. Then she got water for his camels. The man thanked God for helping him.

The servant met Rebekah's family. He told them about Abraham and Isaac. He told how God had helped him find Rebekah.

Rebekah's family loved her. They would miss her. They let her go to marry Isaac. They knew this was what God wanted.

Sometimes you will not know what to do. Ask God to help you. He may use the Bible to show you what to do. He may use other people or things that happen. Be sure to thank God for His help!

You Can Pray:

Dear God, I am so glad You know what is best. Thank You for helping me. (Tell God how you need His help.) In Jesus' name. Amen.

Sinead Mahon   Age 8   Ireland

Let's Talk:

1. How did the servant know which girl to choose for Isaac?
2. What are some ways God may help you know what to do?
3. What choices do you need God to help you make?

14. Twin Brothers

 Have you ever been really hungry? How much would you pay for food? One man in this story was willing to pay a lot!

Isaac loved his wife, Rebekah. He asked God to give her a baby. God gave Rebekah twins!

The first baby was Esau. He had lots of hair. He was the oldest son. He would get most of his father's things someday. That was called a birthright. The second baby was Jacob. The younger son would not get very much.

God's Word Says:
" . . . a prudent [wise] man gives thought to his steps."
Proverbs 14:15

The boys grew up. Esau was a hunter. Jacob took care of things at home. Jacob and Esau did not get along.

 One day Jacob made some food. Esau was very hungry. Jacob would not give him food. Esau had to make a promise. He said he would let Jacob have his birthright. Then Jacob gave him food. Esau did not make a wise choice.

You may want something right now. Maybe you have a friend who wants you to do something wrong. God wants you to stop and think. Ask Him what is best. God can show you what to do.

 You Can Pray:
Dear God, help me stop and think about what is best. Help me do what You want me to do. Thank You for helping me. In Jesus' name. Amen.

Jhonatan Alves Costa   Age 9   Brazil

Let's Talk:

1. What did Isaac ask God for?
2. What did Esau promise to give Jacob?
3. What should you do when you need to make a choice?

15. Isaac Is Tricked

Do you like to trick people? Some tricks are just for fun. Others are bad! Someone played a bad trick on Isaac.

Isaac was old and could not see well. He wanted to bless Esau. He sent him to get food. Then Isaac would ask God to do good things for Esau.

God's Word Says:
"Trust in the LORD and do good. . . ."
Psalm 37:3

Rebekah wanted Jacob to have the blessing. She helped him trick his father. Jacob put on Esau's clothes. He wore goatskins so he would feel hairy like Esau.

Jacob went to his father and said he was Esau. That was wrong! God did not like it.

God does not want you to lie and trick people to get what you want. He wants you to trust Him to work things out.

Jacob did not trust God. He tricked his father. Isaac thought Jacob was really Esau. He gave Jacob the blessing! Jacob would be boss over Esau. His family would be God's people. Other people would serve Jacob.

Esau brought the food for his father. Isaac knew he had been tricked. Esau was very angry! Now Jacob had Esau's birthright and his blessing.

You Can Pray:
Dear God, I am so glad You can make things work out right. Help me trust You and do what is right. In Jesus' name. Amen.

32

Maria   Age 9   India

Let's Talk:

1. Why did Jacob want to trick his father?
2. What blessing Bid Isaac give Jacob?
3. What should you do when you think things will not work out right?

16. Jacob Gets Married

 Do you ever get in trouble? Jacob did! His brother was very angry! Esau wanted to kill Jacob. Jacob had to leave home.

Jacob moved far away. He found out where his uncle lived. Laban was happy to have Jacob live with him.

Laban had two girls—Rachel and Leah. Jacob loved Rachel. He wanted to marry her. He worked for Laban seven years. Now Rachel could be his wife.

Laban tricked Jacob. He made Leah Jacob's wife. Jacob was angry! He did not want to marry Leah! He still loved Rachel. Laban let him marry Rachel too. Jacob had to work seven more years!

> **God's Word Says:**
> " . . . be patient with everyone."
> 1 Thessalonians 5:14

 God was teaching Jacob patience. Patience is waiting calmly for what you want.

God says to be patient with everyone. Maybe you have to wait for your turn. A friend may be slow. You want to hurry. Ask God to help you be patient with everyone.

Jacob worked 14 years for Rachel! God saw that Leah was not loved. He gave her six sons. Rachel did not have any children. God was teaching Rachel to be patient.

You Can Pray:
Dear God, it is hard for me to be patient. (Tell God about times you need His help being patient.) Thank You for helping me. In Jesus' name. Amen.

Jemima Rama   Age 9   Mauritius

Let's Talk:

1. What did Jacob want to do?
2. How did Laban trick Jacob?
3. When do you need to be patient?

17. Jealous Brothers

Have you ever been jealous? A friend gets a new game. You want it. It makes you unhappy. Jacob had some unhappy sons. Why were they jealous?

Many years went by. Jacob was an old man. Then God gave Rachel a son. She named him Joseph. Jacob loved Joseph very much.

Joseph was 17 years old. He and his brothers took care of Jacob's animals. Joseph's brothers did bad things. Maybe they did not work hard. Joseph told his father.

Jacob loved Joseph more than his other sons. He made Joseph a special robe. It was very fancy. The other brothers did not get one.

Joseph's brothers were jealous. They knew their father loved Joseph the best. They hated Joseph. They said mean things to him. This did not make God happy.

Are you jealous of anyone? Do you say mean things? Do you think bad thoughts about him or her? You can ask God to help you. Thank Him for that person. Ask God to help you love him or her. Be sure to thank God for what He has given you.

You Can Pray:
Dear God, I am glad You can help me. (Ask for God's help to love the person you are jealous of.) Thank You for loving me. In Jesus' name. Amen.

Carlos Pereira   Age 10   Angola

Let's Talk:

1. Why do you think Jacob loved Joseph the best?
2. Why were Joseph's brothers jealous?
3. What can you do when you feel jealous?

18. Joseph's Dreams

Has anyone ever been mad at you because you told the truth? That is what happened to Joseph.

Joseph's brothers hated him. They were jealous. Joseph had two dreams that made things worse.

Joseph told the first dream. He and his brothers were in the field. They were tying grain into bunches. Joseph's grain stood up straight. The brothers' grain bowed down to his grain. When his brothers heard this, they hated Joseph even more.

Joseph told about his other dream. The moon, sun and 11 stars bowed to him. The moon and sun were like Joseph's parents. The stars were like his brothers. Joseph's father heard this. He scolded Joseph. "Will your mother and I and your brothers bow down to you?"

Joseph had told the truth about his dreams. His family was angry. There may be times when people are angry because you tell the truth. Maybe you see someone hurt another person. You need to tell the truth about what happened. Then it can be stopped. Ask God to show you when to tell what you know.

You Can Pray:
Dear God, thank You that You are with me. Please help me not be afraid to tell the truth. In Jesus' name. Amen.

This Bible story can be found in Genesis 37:5-11.

Loren   Age 10   Cote d'Ivoire

Let's Talk:
1. What did Joseph do that made his brothers angry?
2. What did Joseph's dreams mean?
3. Why should you tell the truth about things that happen?

19. Trouble for Joseph

 Do you ever get angry? Does it make you do bad things? Joseph's brothers were very angry! It made them do something wrong.

Joseph's father sent him to find his brothers. They were watching the sheep. They saw Joseph coming. They wanted to kill him.

God's Word Says:
"In your anger do not sin. . . ."
Psalm 4:4

The brothers took off Joseph's beautiful robe. They threw him into a big hole. The brothers saw some traders coming. They did not kill Joseph. They sold him as a slave. The brothers put blood on his robe. They told their father that Joseph was dead.

What a bad thing to do! Getting angry is not always wrong. But when anger makes you do bad things, it is sin. Ask God to help you when you are angry. He can give you strength to do what is right. God can help you forgive and love others.

Joseph's brothers sold him. The traders took him to Egypt. A man named Potiphar bought Joseph to be his slave. God was still with him. He helped him do well in Egypt. Potiphar put Joseph in charge of all that he owned.

 You Can Pray:
Dear God, (tell God about things that make you angry). Help me not to sin when I am angry. Help me to love others and do what is right. In Jesus' name. Amen.

Jenya Tsarenko   Age 7   Russia

Let's Talk:

1. What did Joseph's brothers do to him?
2. What did God do for Joseph while he was in Egypt?
3. How can God help you when you are angry?

20. Joseph Is Tempted

 Has anyone tried to get you to do something wrong? That is being tempted. Joseph had that happen. He was still a slave at Potiphar's house.

God blessed Joseph. He did his job well. Potiphar put Joseph in charge of all that he owned. He took care of things. Potiphar trusted him.

Joseph was good-looking. Potiphar's wife liked him. She wanted Joseph to do wrong things with her. He knew that would not please God. He said, "No!"

God's Word Says:
" . . . God is faithful; . . . when you are tempted, he will also provide a way out. . . ."
1 Corinthians 10:13

 You need to be like Joseph. Say no to temptation. You do not have to sin. God says He will give you a way out. Ask Him to help you do what is right.

Potiphar's wife tempted Joseph day after day. He tried not to be near her. One day they were in the house alone. She caught Joseph by his coat. He left the coat and ran away.

You Can Pray:
Dear God, thank You for making a way out of temptation. (Tell God about things you are tempted to do.) Please help me to do right. In Jesus' name. Amen.

Bekkah Neigh   Age 9   New York

Let's Talk:

1. Who tempted Joseph to do wrong?
2. Why didn't Joseph want to do fwhat she gasked?
3. What can you do when you are tempted?

21. Joseph in Prison

What would it be like to be in prison? Joseph was in prison. He had not done anything wrong! God blessed him in prison. He was put in charge.

Pharaoh was the ruler of Egypt. Two of his helpers were in prison with Joseph. One night they both had dreams. They wanted to know what the dreams meant.

God showed Joseph the meaning of the dreams. The first man was going to get out of prison in three days. He would get his old job back. The second man would die in three days.

God's Word Says:
"I waited patiently for the LORD; he turned to me and heard my cry."
Psalm 40:1

Both dreams came true just as Joseph said. Joseph had asked the first man to tell Pharaoh about him. The man forgot. Joseph had to stay in prison two more years!

Do you think Joseph got tired of waiting? Yes he did. Still he knew God would work things out. He just had to be patient.

You may have to wait for God to work too. Maybe you have a problem at home or at school. Keep praying. Ask God to take care of it. Then be patient while you wait.

You Can Pray:
Dear God, thank You for always being with me. Help me tell You about my problems. Then help me wait for You to answer. In Jesus' name. Amen.

Audrey C. Borges Pereira   Age 10   Brazil

Let's Talk:

1. What did the two men want Joseph to do?
2. How did Joseph know what the dreams meant?
3. What should you do while you wait for God to help you?

22. Pharaoh's Dreams

 Do bad things ever happen to you? Joseph had bad things happen! He was still in jail. Two more years went by.

Pharaoh had a dream about seven fat cows. Seven skinny cows ate the fat ones! Then Pharaoh dreamed about seven good heads of grain. Seven thin ones ate the good ones.

God's Word Says:
" . . . in all things God works for the good of those who love him. . . ."
Romans 8:28

Pharaoh wanted to know what the dreams meant. No one could tell him. His helper remembered about Joseph in jail. Pharaoh sent for him. God showed Joseph what the dreams meant. For seven years there would be a lot of food. Then there would be seven years without food.

 Pharaoh needed a wise helper. He chose Joseph to be in charge! Joseph helped the people save food in the good years. They would eat that food in the bad years. God had worked things out for Joseph in a good way.

You need to trust God like Joseph did. Talk to Him. Obey Him during good and bad times. God will work things out the best way. He may reward you with good things now. He will also reward you in Heaven.

 You Can Pray:
Dear God, help me trust You when bad things happen. I know You will work things out and reward me at the right time. In Jesus' name. Amen.

Wade Johns   Age 8   Missouri

Let's Talk:

1. How did Pharaoh hear about Joseph?
2. What did the dreams mean?
3. What can you do to earn rewards from God?

23. Joseph Forgives

? What if someone is mean to you? Do you stay angry and want to punish that person? Do you forgive him or her? Find out what Joseph did.

Joseph was in charge in Egypt. The seven good years had passed. Now there were seven bad years. People came from all over to buy food from Joseph.

God's Word Says:
" . . . Forgive as the Lord forgave you."
Colossians 3:13

Joseph's brothers came for food. They did not know him. He looked different. Joseph tested his brothers. He told them to bring their youngest brother back. They did not want to do it.

Finally all the brothers came back to Egypt. Joseph could tell they had changed. They were sorry for selling him as a slave. Joseph told his brothers who he was. He forgave them for the things they had done.

God wants you to forgive those who hurt you too. Ask God to give you love for them, not anger. It will help them. You will feel better too. You will know you are pleasing God.

Joseph pleased God by forgiving his brothers. God took the bad things that happened and worked them out for good.

You Can Pray:
Dear God, thank You for forgiving me. Help me love and forgive like You do. (Tell God about someone you need to forgive.) In Jesus' name. Amen.

This Bible story can be found in Genesis 42—45:8.

Rebecca Bischoff   Age 10   Missouri

Let's Talk:
1. Why did people come to see Joseph?
2. How do you think Joseph's brothers felt when he told them who he was?
3. What does God say about forgiving others?

24. Joseph's Family

 Have you ever heard of a famine? It is a time when food will not grow. People are hungry. There are famines today like there were in Joseph's time.

There was a famine where Joseph's family lived. It would last five more years. Joseph wanted to take care of his family.

Joseph told his brothers to go home and tell his father he was alive. He sent gifts with them. Joseph wanted the whole family to move to Egypt.

Jacob was surprised and happy to hear about Joseph! He thought Joseph had been killed. Jacob was thankful God had saved Joseph. Jacob and Joseph's brothers moved to Egypt. The family grew bigger and bigger. God was with them.

Bad things had happened to Joseph. He still did what God wanted. He trusted God. Now God could use Joseph to take care of his family. They were God's people.

Hard times can come in your life. Things happen you do not understand. Keep trusting God. He has a plan for your life. He can make things work out right. He did that for Joseph.

You Can Pray:
Dear God, thank You that You have a plan for my life. Help me trust You to make things work out right. In Jesus' name. Amen.

This Bible story can be found in Genesis 45:9—47:27.

Emmie Neigh   Age 6   New York

Let's Talk:
1. Why did Joseph's family need to leave their home?
2. How did God's plan for Joseph help his family?
3. What can you trust God to do for you?

25. Baby Moses

Can God take care of you all the time? God can take care of anyone—even a tiny baby.

The new king of Egypt did not know about Joseph. He did not love God. He made God's people slaves. They had to work very hard without pay. The king made a terrible rule. Every new baby boy had to be thrown in the river to drown!

God's Word Says:
"The LORD is good. . . . He cares for those who trust in him."
Nahum 1:7

One mother hid her baby so he would not be killed. She put him in a basket in the river. Miriam was the baby's sister. She watched to see what would happen.

God was taking care of the baby. The king's daughter found him in the river. She wanted to keep the baby. She named him Moses. The king's daughter needed help taking care of him. Miriam's mother was able to take care of her own baby! That was God's plan!

God loves you like He loved baby Moses. He is taking care of you. Maybe you are having a problem at school. Maybe something scares you. The Bible says you can trust God to take care of you!

You Can Pray:
Dear God, thank You for loving me and taking care of me. (Tell God about your problem. Ask Him to help you.) In Jesus' name. Amen.

Ashley Irelan   Age 7   Alabama

Let's Talk:

1. How did God take care of baby Moses?
2. What is one way God has taken care of you?
3. What should you remember when you have a problem?

26. Moses Meets the King

 Can you think of someone who has great power? God has more power than anyone does! One day a king learned how powerful God is.

Moses was now an adult. He lived far away from Egypt. God's people were still slaves in Egypt. They prayed for God's help. God heard their prayers. He picked Moses to help them.

Moses and his brother went to see the king. They told him, "God said, 'Let my people go!'" The king said, "No!" Moses warned the king that bad things would happen.

 God caused the water in the rivers to turn into blood. God made lots of frogs cover the land. God caused many flies to bother the people and their animals.

God has power over everything. He has power over the Earth, the animals and even tiny insects. No one is more powerful than God is. Have you ever thanked God for His great power?

The king saw God's power. Still he would not let God's people go free. Moses warned the king that soon more bad things would happen.

You Can Pray:
Dear God, thank You for Your mighty power. Thank You for loving me. Thank You for taking care of me. In Jesus' name. Amen.

David Hargrove   Age 9   California

Let's Talk:

1. Why do you think the king of Egypt would not let God's people go free?
2. How did God show His power to the king?
3. What are some other powerful things God can do?

27. More Plagues

Do you know what a warning is? It means that you must be careful or something bad might happen. Moses gave the king a warning. Would he listen?

The king still kept God's people as slaves in Egypt. Can you remember some of the bad things that happened in Egypt? Soon more bad things happened!

God made the animals and people sick. God sent a big storm that hurt everything growing in the fields. God sent insects that ate the fruit from the trees. God sent terrible darkness that covered the land day and night.

Each time God asked the king to change his mind. The king would not. He thought he was stronger than God was. No one is stronger than God is. God is in charge of everything and everyone.

God is in charge of you. It is important to listen to God's warnings. God loves you. He always tells the truth. You can believe God. The king would not believe God and listen to Him. Soon the worst thing of all was going to happen!

You Can Pray:
Dear God, thank You for loving me. Help me listen to You. Help me believe what You say. Thank You for always telling me the truth. In Jesus' name. Amen.

This Bible story can be found in Exodus 9:1—10:29.

Angelina Mollozzi   Age 9   New York

Let's Talk:
1. What happened when the king would not listen to God's warning?
2. What is God in charge of?
3. Why should you listen to God and believe Him?

28. Delivered from Egypt

 Why were bad things happening in Egypt? God told the king to set His people free. The king said, "No!" Now what would happen?

Moses gave the king a final warning. The oldest child in each family would die that night if the king did not change his mind. Still the king said, "No!"

God told His people to get ready. A lamb was killed for each family. The lambs' blood was spread around the door of each house. Then no one in the houses would die. The lambs died instead.

God's Word Says: "You have been set free from sin. . . ." Romans 6:18

 That night God's people were safe because they believed God. However, the oldest child in each Egyptian family died. Even the king's child died. Now the king said, "Go!" God's people were finally free! They quickly packed their things and left Egypt.

God told His people to always remember this night. It was a picture of what the Lord Jesus would do later. Jesus would come to Earth to bleed and die on the cross for your sin. You can be free from your sin if you believe in Jesus.

 You Can Pray:
Dear God, thank You for Jesus, who died for me. Thank You that He took my punishment so I can be free from my sin. In Jesus' name. Amen

Rebeca Esteves   Age 10   Missouri

Let's Talk:

1. What was God's final warning for the king?
2. What did God's people do so no one in their houses would die?
3. What do you have to do so you can be free from your sin?

29. Triumphant Crossing

? Does God know and care when bad things happen to you? Did He care about His people? Soon after they left Egypt, the king changed his mind!

The people followed Moses into the desert. God sent a special cloud to guide them. God wanted them to remember that He was in control!

God's Word Says:
" . . . we trust in the name of the LORD our God."
Psalm 20:7

God's people came to the edge of the sea. Then they saw that the king's army was chasing them! Where could they go? They were afraid! Moses told them to trust God to take care of them.

You can trust God to take care of you. Even when bad things happen, God is still in control. He knows and cares about you. He will do what is best for you.

God took care of His people. He sent a strong wind that pushed the water apart. All God's people walked safely across to the other side. The king's army tried to follow. God made the water pour back over the army.

God's people were happy and praised God. They thanked Him for His power and His control.

You Can Pray:
Thank You, God for Your power and control. Thank You that You know and care about me. Help me to trust You when bad things happen. In Jesus' name. Amen.

This Bible story can be found in Exodus 13:17—14:31.

Curtis Evers   Age 8   Tennessee

Let's Talk:

1. How did God show His people that He was in control?
2. How do you know that God cares about you?
3. What should you remember when something bad happens?

30. God Provides

Does God know what you need? Can you trust Him to give it to you? God's people needed to learn that God would take care of all their needs.

The people were now safe from their enemies. They walked into the desert. Soon they were thirsty. The water they found was not good to drink. The people complained to Moses. Moses prayed. God showed him how to make the water clean.

God's Word Says:
"And my God will meet all your needs . . . in Christ Jesus."
Philippians 4:19

Later the people became hungry. They complained to Moses again. Moses prayed. God sent them special bread called manna. He also sent many birds called quail for the people to catch and eat.

Did the people learn a lesson? No! Later when they were thirsty they complained again. Complaining does not please God. It shows you are not trusting God to take care of you. God wants you to be thankful for what He gives you.

Every day for 40 years God made sure His people had what they needed. Still they grumbled and complained. Do not be like them! Say thank You to God every day for all He does for you.

You Can Pray:
Dear God, thank You for giving me all that I need. Help me not to complain. Help me always to be thankful. In Jesus' name. Amen.

Cathy Cunningham   Age 9   Oregon

Let's Talk:

1. What did God's people complain about?
2. What does God want you to do instead of complaining?
3. What are some things you can thank God for?

31. God Visits His People

? What if an important visitor was coming to your house? Would you clean your room or change your clothes? God was about to visit His people!

God's Word Says:
". . . Be holy because I, the LORD your God, am holy."
Leviticus 19:2

God's people camped near a big mountain. Moses climbed up the mountain to meet with God. God said that He was going to come down in a thick cloud. He would talk to the people.

God said His people should clean and get ready. Why did they have to do this? God is holy. He is clean from any sinful thing. God wants His people to be holy too. It is not enough to be clean on the outside. He wants them to be clean on the inside.

God wants you to be clean on the inside too. Be clean from thinking sinful thoughts. Be clean from saying sinful words. Be clean from doing sinful things.

How can you be clean on the inside? Tell God about your sin. Ask Him to help you do right. Ask God to make you holy like He is.

God's people were clean and ready to meet Him!

You Can Pray:
Dear God, I want to always be ready to meet with You. Please help me stay clean on the inside so I can be like You. In Jesus' name. Amen.

Cierra Dunn   Age 7   Oregon

Let's Talk:

1. Why did God's people have to prepare to meet with Him?
2. What does it mean that God is holy?
3. How can you be clean on the inside?

32. God's Rules

Can others tell that you love God? God wants you to love Him with all your heart. He has given some important ways you can do that.

God's people saw a thick cloud on the mountain. Thunder boomed and lightning flashed. God had come! The people were afraid. Then God gave them ten rules. The first four rules would show that they loved Him.

God's Word Says:
" . . . Love the Lord your God with all your heart. . . ."
Luke 10:27

God said, "Do not worship any other gods, only Me. Do not make statues to worship in place of Me. Do not use My name in a bad way. Keep one day every week to rest and worship Me."

Are you keeping these rules? Do you worship only God? Do you make sure that no person or thing is more important to you than God? Do you use God's name only in a respectful way? Do you take time to rest and worship God each week? These things will show others that you love God with all your heart.

God wants you to love Him. He also wants you to love others. That is what the next four rules are about.

You Can Pray:
Dear God, I love You with all my heart. Please help me obey the rules You have given. I want to show my love for You. In Jesus' name. Amen.

Sarah Baer   Age 7   Ohio

Let's Talk:

1. What are the first four rules God gave on the mountain?
2. What does it mean to love God with all your heart?
3. What are some ways you can show your love for God this week?

33. Loving Other People

Can you guess the two most important things God wants you to learn? You know the first one. Love God with all your heart. Now let's talk about the second one.

God's people were at the mountain. They listened carefully to Him. Can you remember God's first four rules? Here are the next four.

God's Word Says:
" . . . Love your neighbor as [you love] yourself."
Matthew 22:39

God said, "Treat your parents with respect. Do not kill. Married people must keep their promises to each other. Do not take things that belong to someone else."

These rules remind you to love other people. You should show respect for them. God is perfect. Loving Him is easy. People are not perfect. Sometimes it is hard to love them. Loving people is the second most important thing God wants you to learn!

God says you are to love others just like you love yourself. That means treat them kindly. Take care of them. Do nice things for them. Treat other people just like you want to be treated. That is not easy to do. You need God's help to do it!

You Can Pray:
Dear God, I want to keep Your rules by loving other people. Please help me to treat others the way I want to be treated. In Jesus' name. Amen.

Scott Weir   Age 9   Missouri

Let's Talk:

1. What four rules have you learned today?
2. How much are you to love other people?
3. What are some ways you can show your love to others?

34. Two More Rules

Have you ever told a lie? Have you ever wanted something that was not yours? If so, you have broken two of God's rules!

God's people listened carefully to Him. What were His first eight rules? These rules help you remember to love God and love others.

God has two more rules to help you show your love for Him and for others. God said, "Do not tell lies. Do not want things that belong to others."

Lying to others does not show love. You should love others like you love yourself. Then you will always tell them the truth.

Maybe you really want what someone else has. You may even cry or fuss to get what you want. God said if you truly love Him, you should be happy with what He gives you.

God's ten rules show how sinful you are. They are called the Ten Commandments. No one can keep these rules without God's help. God is ready to help you. Just ask Him!

Will God's people keep His rules? Will they obey Him? Will you?

You Can Pray:
Dear God, please help me tell the truth. Make me happy with what You give me. Please help me keep all of Your rules. In Jesus' name. Amen.

Diana Beke   Age 7   Oregon

Let's Talk:

1. Why should you tell the truth?
2. Why should you be happy with what God gives you?
3. What can you do when it is hard to keep all of God's rules?

35. The Golden Calf

 Have you ever broken a promise? Keeping promises to others is important. It is really important to keep your promises to God.

God's people had promised to keep His rules. God called Moses to meet Him on the mountain. Moses stayed there for a long time. He watched God write His rules on stone.

God's Word Says:
" . . .I have promised to obey your words."
Psalm 119:57

The people did not think Moses would come back. They asked his brother to make them a god they could see. Moses' brother made a calf from gold. The people worshiped the golden calf. They did not keep their promise to worship only God.

 Have you made promises to God? Have you promised to obey Him? Have you promised to talk to Him every day? Do not forget your promises! God will not forget them. Ask God to help you do what you say you will.

God's people did not keep their promises. God was angry. Moses was angry too. Moses broke the stone with God's rules. He broke the golden calf. God punished the people for their sins. He wanted the people to remember to keep their promises to Him.

 You Can Pray:
Dear God, help me remember that my promises to You are important. Help me to do what I say I will do. In Jesus' name. Amen.

This Bible story can be found in Exodus 32:1-30; 34:1-4.

Maja Cieptowska   Age 10   Poland

Let's Talk:

1. What did Moses do on the mountain?
2. How did God's people break their promise to Him?
3. Why is it important to keep your promises to God?

36. The Twelve Spies

 What does it mean to believe God? It means to trust that He will do what He says. God's people had to decide if they would believe God.

They finally came to the land God had promised to give them. Moses chose 12 men to go see what it was like. The 12 spies went. After 40 days they came back. They brought a big bunch of grapes that took two men to carry!

> **God's Word Says:**
> "When I am afraid, I will trust in you [God]."
> Psalm 56:3

Ten of the spies said, "It is a good land but the people who live there are strong. We cannot win over them." God's people were afraid! Joshua and Caleb were the other two spies. They said, "Do not be afraid! Believe God. He will help us win!"

It can be hard to believe God when you are afraid. Remember that God knows what is happening to you. If you are His child, He is always with you. Trust God to do what He says. Then obey Him!

The people had to decide. Would they believe God or the ten spies?

> **You Can Pray:**
> Dear God, thank You that You always do what You say. Help me to believe You and obey even when I am afraid. In Jesus' name. Amen.

This Bible story can be found in Numbers 13:1-2, 17—14:9.

Christie Trimble   Age 7   Arizona

Let's Talk:

1. What did Joshua and Caleb say to God's people?
2. What does it mean to believe God?
3. What should you remember when you are afraid?

37. In the Desert

 Do you know people who always want their own way? Do you sometimes want your own way? What does God have to say about that?

God's people had come to the land that God had for them. Do you remember what the first ten spies said? What did Joshua and Caleb say? What would the people do?

God's Word Says:
"As for God, his way is perfect. . . ."
2 Samuel 22:31

The Bible says the people complained. They did not believe God. They believed the ten spies. They would not go into the land. These people wanted their own way, not God's way.

 Wanting your own way is sin. It shows that you do not believe God. God's way is always best. What is God's way? Obey your parents. Be kind to others. Tell the truth. Have you been doing things your way or God's way?

God was angry with His people. He would have to punish them. They would travel in the desert for 40 more years! By then all the adults who came out of Egypt would die. Then their children could enter the land.

Do not be like those people. Believe God and follow His way.

 You Can Pray:
Dear God, I am sorry for the times I want my own way. Help me to remember that Your way is always best. In Jesus' name. Amen.

This Bible story can be found in Numbers 14:10-38.

Emily Caran   Age 9   Missouri

Let's Talk:

1. Why did God's people choose their own way?
2. Why is God's way always best?
3. What are some things you know are God's way?

38. A New Leader

Have you ever had a hard job to do? Were you afraid you would not be able to do it? That is how Joshua felt!

Forty years had passed. God's people were finally ready to go into the land God had for them. Moses had died. Joshua would be their new leader.

There were almost two million people for Joshua to lead into a land full of enemies! How would he be able to do it? God said to Joshua, "Do not be afraid." Then He told Joshua that He would be with him and would help him.

God says the same thing to you. If you are His child, He is with you all the time. Do not be afraid. He will help you in everything you do. Tell God about that hard job you have to do. Trust Him to help you.

Joshua had courage knowing that God was with him. He reminded the people to obey God's Word and trust in Him. Leading these people was going to be a big job. With God's help Joshua knew he could do it!

You Can Pray:
Dear God, thank You for being with me all the time. (Tell God about a hard job you have to do.) In Jesus' name. Amen.

Briana Chui   Age 7   Oregon

Let's Talk:

1. What big job did Joshua have to do?
2. What did God tell Joshua that gave him courage?
3. What should you remember when you have a hard job to do?

39. Rahab and the Spies

 Have you ever been in danger? Maybe a big storm is coming. You need a plan to be safe. A lady in the Bible needed a plan to be safe.

Joshua led God's people to Jericho. The people there were their enemies. The city had a big strong wall around it.

Joshua sent in two spies. A woman named Rahab lived in a house right on the wall. She invited the spies into her house. The king found out about the spies. He sent soldiers to catch them.

> **God's Word Says:**
> "For I know the plans I have for you, declares [says] the LORD. . . ."
> Jeremiah 29:11

Rahab hid the spies. The soldiers could not find them. Rahab helped the spies. She believed in their powerful God. God used Rahab in His plan to save the spies.

God has good plans for you too. He may use people in His plan. He may use other things to help you. You can always trust God's plan for you.

Rahab let the spies down through her window on a rope. They told her God's plan. They told her to place a red cord in her window for safety in the battle. Would Rahab trust God's plan?

 You Can Pray:
Dear God, thank You that You have good plans for me. Help me to trust Your plan. In Jesus' name. Amen.

Clarissa Mosley   Age 7   Oregon

Let's Talk:

1. How did Rahab help the spies?
2. What was God's plan for Rahab?
3. Why should you trust God's plan for you?

40. The Fall of Jericho

 How would you knock down a big wall? Joshua had a big wall in front of him. God had a strange plan to knock it down!

Jericho had a strong wall. God wanted His people to take the city away from the enemy. He told Joshua, "March around the city once a day for six days. On the next day march around it seven times. Then blow the trumpets and shout. The wall will fall down."

God's Word Says:
" . . . be strong in the Lord and in his mighty power."
Ephesians 6:10

God's people could only win over their enemy with God's help and power. As God's child you have an enemy too. His name is Satan. He wants you to think, say and do bad things.

You can only win over Satan with God's help and power. Tell God when you are tempted to do something that is bad. Ask Him to help you say no and do what is right. God will help you win over your enemy.

God's people wanted to win in Jericho. They did what God said. They marched and marched. They blew the trumpets and shouted. The wall fell down! Now the battle could begin.

You Can Pray:
Dear God, sometimes I am tempted to do bad things. Please help me and give me the power to do what is right. In Jesus' name. Amen.

This Bible story can be found in Joshua 5:13—6:11.

Gabriel Yee   Age 8   California

Let's Talk:
1. What was God's strange plan to knock down the wall of Jericho?
2. What kind of bad things does Satan tempt you to do?
3. How can you win over Satan?

41. Rahab Is Saved

 When people are in trouble, what do they do? They look for a way to escape! Rahab was in trouble. Would she be able to escape?

God had caused Jericho's wall to fall. His people were ready to take over the city. Joshua remembered Rahab. What had she done for God's people?

God's Word Says:
". . . While we were still sinners, Christ died for us."
Romans 5:8

Joshua told the two spies to bring Rahab and her family out. How did they find her? She had put the red cord in her window. The men brought her to safety. Rahab believed God. He made a way for her to escape. She was not punished with the others in her city.

God made a way for all people to escape being punished for sin. That way is to believe in His Son, Jesus. He died on the cross. He was punished for your sin. He was buried. Then He came alive again.

If you have believed in the Lord Jesus Christ, you will not be punished. Do you know others who need to believe in Jesus? Tell them about the way of escape God has made for them.

 You Can Pray:
Dear God, thank You for Jesus, who died so I will not have to be punished for my sin. Help me to tell others about Him. In Jesus' name. Amen.

Michael Spracklin   Age 7   New Brunswick, Canada

Let's Talk:

1. What did Rahab do that showed she trusted God?
2. How can you be saved from your sin?
3. What can you tell someone else who needs to believe in the Lord Jesus?

42. Deborah and Barak

Have you played follow the leader? It is fun to be the leader. God wants you to show others the right thing to do.

After Joshua died, God's people sinned. They did not obey God. He let enemies win over them. God sent leaders to show them what to do.

One of those leaders was Deborah. God gave Deborah a message for Barak. He led the army. God said Barak was to take his army to the top of a mountain. God would do the rest! Barak asked Deborah to go along.

The enemy stood at the bottom of the mountain. Deborah was not afraid. "Go!" she said to Barak. She trusted God. She showed Barak the right thing to do.

Do you show people the right thing to do? Do you trust God and help others trust Him too?

Barak's army ran down the mountain. The leader of the enemy was so scared he left his chariot! God's people won the battle! Do you think Barak was glad he did what Deborah said? Barak and Deborah and all the people gave thanks to God.

You Can Pray:
Dear God, thank You for those who show me the right things to do. Help me show others what to do too. In Jesus' name. Amen.

Landon Hart   Age 7   Oregon

Let's Talk:

1. What message did God have for Barak?
2. How did Deborah show Barak the right thing to do?
3. How can God use you to show others the right things to do?

43. Gideon Is Chosen

 Do you know what it means to be bold? It means to be brave and do what is right. Gideon needed to be bold.

God had helped Deborah to win a great battle for His people. After she died, God's people broke their promise to Him. They started to worship other gods. God had to punish them again.

Enemies came through their land. They were the Midianites. They stole food and animals and wrecked the land. God's people were afraid. One of those people was a farmer named Gideon. He hid as he did his work.

 An angel came. He said that God had chosen Gideon to lead His people against their enemy. "I am not strong enough to do this!" Gideon said. He did not feel bold! God promised to be with him and help him.

God wants you to be bold for Him. Maybe you are afraid to do what God says. God is with you. He can give you courage to obey Him. When you feel afraid, ask God to make you bold!

God was ready to help Gideon be bold.

 You Can Pray:
Dear God, sometimes I feel afraid to obey You. Please help me be bold and do what You say. In Jesus' name. Amen.

Andrew Rasmussen   Age 10   Denmark

Let's Talk:

1. Why was Gideon afraid?
2. What does it mean to be bold?
3. What can you do when you need to be bold?

44. Gideon's Battle

Have you ever been on a team? What if your team is much smaller than the other team? That is what happened to Gideon.

There were 135,000 in the enemy army. There were only 32,000 in Gideon's army. Then God sent most of Gideon's army home. He only had 300 men left!

God's Word Says:
"I can do everything through him who gives me strength."
Philippians 4:13

How could they win against such a big enemy? God knew that His people could not win this battle. That is why He sent so many of Gideon's men home. They would have to trust God to help them.

You may feel alone trying to be bold for God. No one else seems to obey Him. God does not want you to count on your own strength. He wants you to trust Him to help you. That is what He wanted Gideon to do.

God told Gideon to take trumpets, jars and torches. His men stood outside the enemy camp. Gideon gave a signal. They blew the trumpets and broke the jars. Now the torches could shine. The enemy was so afraid they all ran away. God's people had won!

You Can Pray:
Dear God, I need Your strength to obey. Thank You for helping me trust in You. In Jesus' name. Amen.

This Bible story can be found in Judges 7:1-25; 8:22-28.

Adam Caran   Age 8   Missouri

Let's Talk:

1. Why did God send so many of Gideon's men home?
2. How did Gideon's army win the battle?
3. What do you need to do when you feel alone in serving God?

45. King Saul Disobeys

Do you always obey all that God says? God once gave a king an important job to do. Would the king obey?

King Saul was the king of Israel. God sent a man named Samuel. He gave King Saul a job to do. God wanted Saul to attack an enemy country. God told him to make sure everything was destroyed.

King Saul took his army and attacked the enemy. They destroyed *almost* everything. Saul saved the enemy king and the best animals. Saul was proud of what he had done. Had he obeyed all that God said? No!

Do you obey all that God says? God says to tell the truth. Do you only tell part of the truth? God says to be kind to everybody. Are you kind only to those who are nice to you? It is not always easy to obey God completely. When you do, it shows that you love Him. Ask God to help you obey Him.

King Saul did not ask for God's help. God was angry. He said He would choose someone else to be king.

You Can Pray:
Dear God, I am sorry for times I did not obey You. Please help me do everything You tell me. In Jesus' name. Amen.

samuel

King Saul

Matt Baer   Age 9   Ohio

Let's Talk:

1. What job did God give King Saul to do?
2. What did God say would happen because King Saul disobeyed?
3. What can you do when you are tempted not to obey completely?

46. God Chooses David

 What would you look for if you had to choose a king? What kind of person would God choose to be the new king in Israel?

Saul had not obeyed God completely. God sent Samuel to find a new king. He went to Jesse's house. Jesse had eight sons. Which one would God choose?

God's Word Says:
" . . . Man looks at the outward appearance, but the LORD looks at the heart."
1 Samuel 16:7

 The oldest son was tall and looked good. *This must be the one!* Samuel thought. God said, "No." God told Samuel, "You see what he looks like on the outside. I see what he is like on the inside." God wanted a king who would love and obey Him.

It does not matter if you are short or tall. It does not matter what color eyes or skin you have. God cares about what you are like on the inside. He wants people who will love and obey Him.

None of the sons Samuel saw was the right one. Then Jesse sent for his youngest son, David. God said, "This is the one!" God knew David would be a good king who would love and obey Him.

 You Can Pray:
Dear God, please help me be the kind of person You would choose to serve You. Help me love and obey You. In Jesus' name. Amen.

This Bible story can be found in 1 Samuel 16:1-13.

Sarah Menhart   Age 9   Washington

Let's Talk:

1. Why did Samuel think the oldest son would be a good king?
2. What did God tell Samuel about choosing the right person?
3. How can you be the kind of person God chooses to serve Him?

47. David and Goliath

Have you ever had a really big problem? God's people did. Their problem was a giant named Goliath.

"Send a man to fight me!" Goliath shouted every day in his big booming voice. He made fun of God's people. No one wanted to fight him. They were afraid!

David came to the army camp. He heard the giant's words. He said, "I will fight this giant!" How could David do this? He was not big or strong enough. "God will help me!" David said. He was trusting God to help him with this problem.

God is willing to help you with your problems. He knows you are not strong enough to take care of them by yourself. God can solve even the biggest problems. Remember that God is with you. Tell Him about the problem. He is always there to help you.

David knew God was there to help him. David put a stone in his sling and ran to the giant. He threw the stone and hit the giant in the head. The giant fell down. God had helped David kill the enemy.

You Can Pray:
Dear God, thank You for always being with me. (Tell Him about a big problem you have.) Thank You for helping me with this problem. In Jesus' name. Amen.

Rachel Roberts   Age 9   Oregon

Let's Talk:

1. What big problem did David have?
2. How did David know he could win over the giant?
3. What should you do when you have a big problem?

48. David and Jonathan

? Do you have a best friend? David did! David's best friend was a prince!

After he killed the giant, David went to live in the palace. King Saul lived there. His son Prince Jonathan lived there too. Jonathan gave David gifts. He gave him his robe, his belt and his own sword.

David and Jonathan promised to always be kind to each other. They would be kind to each other's families too. Jonathan was David's best friend. Jonathan believed in God. Jonathan was kind. David knew he could trust Jonathan to keep his promise.

It is good to have many friends. Your best friend should be special. Your best friend should be someone who is God's child. Your best friend should be someone who is kind. Your best friend should be someone you can trust.

Ask God to give you a special best friend. Ask God to help you be a good best friend too. You need to be kind and keep your promises.

David chose a good best friend. David and Jonathan always kept their promises to each other.

You Can Pray:
Dear God, thank You for my friends. Please help me choose a good best friend. In Jesus' name. Amen.

Victoria Papez   Age 6   Missouri

Let's Talk:

1. How did Jonathan show kindness to David?
2. What did David and Jonathan promise to each other?
3. What should your best friend be like?

49. Saul's Jealousy

Do you get angry if someone else gets something you want? That is called jealousy. King Saul had a problem with jealousy.

David was a brave leader in the king's army. They won many battles when he led them. The people loved David. They made up songs about him. This made King Saul jealous. He wanted the people to cheer for him.

God's Word Says:
"Always giving thanks to God the Father for everything. . . ."
Ephesians 5:20

The king was so jealous he tried to kill David! David was able to get away. The king tried again and again to kill David. Jonathan told David he would never be safe in the palace. He would have to leave.

Jealousy can make you do terrible things. You may say or do something mean. Jealousy does not please God. He wants you to be happy with what you have. Think of all God has given to you and thank Him.

The king never learned to be happy with what he had. David had to leave his best friend. Jealousy caused them all many problems. Ask God to help you be happy and not jealous.

You Can Pray:
Dear God, I am sorry for the times I have been jealous. Help me be happy and thankful for all You have given me. In Jesus' name. Amen.

This Bible story can be found in 1 Samuel 18:5-16; 19:1-42.

Sophia Bempah   Age 9   Ghana

Let's Talk:

1. Why was King Saul jealous of David?
2. What problems did jealousy cause for David and Jonathan?
3. What can you do when you start to feel jealous?

50. Mephibosheth

Do you remember the promise that David and Jonathan made to each other? David was soon going to be able to keep that promise!

King Saul and Jonathan were killed in battle. David became king. David remembered his promise to always show kindness to Jonathan's family.

Jonathan's son Mephibosheth was still alive. He had been hurt when he was a little boy. He could not walk. Now he was an adult. He lived far away from the palace.

David had his servant bring Mephibosheth to him. The young man was afraid of the new king. David said, "Do not be afraid. I will show you kindness because of your father." God was pleased with David's kindness.

Are you kind to other people? Are you kind to your parents and teachers? Are you kind when you play with your friends? Are you kind to your brothers and sisters? God has shown His kindness to you. Now he wants you to be kind to others.

David was kind to Jonathan's son. From then on, Mephibosheth lived in the palace and ate at the king's table.

You Can Pray:
Dear God, thank You for Your kindness to me. Please help me be kind to other people. In Jesus' name. Amen.

This Bible story can be found in 2 Samuel 4:4; 9:1-13.

Kaley Geyer   Age 10   Florida

Let's Talk:
1. How was David kind to Mephibosheth?
2. Who are some people you can be kind to?
3. What are some kind things you can do for others?

51. Esther the Queen

 Is it easy to obey? What about when you do not understand why you should obey? Esther had a choice to make about obeying.

The king of Persia needed a queen. He had a beauty contest. He would choose the most beautiful girl to become his queen. A Jewish girl named Esther was chosen to be in this contest.

God's Word Says:
" . . . Obey me. . . . Walk in all the ways I command you, that it may go well with you."
Jeremiah 7:23

Esther lived with her cousin Mordecai. He told Esther not to tell anyone that she was a Jew. Esther might not have understood but she obeyed him.

The women spent many days getting ready. They wanted to look beautiful for the king. The king liked Esther best. He fell in love with her. He crowned her queen. This was part of God's plan for Esther's life.

God has a plan for your life. You can find His plan in the Bible. He wants you to obey Him. His plans are best. There may be times when you do not understand God's plans for you. You should obey Him anyway. You can trust God. He knows what He is doing.

 You Can Pray:
Dear God, I know that Your plans are best. Help me obey even when I do not understand. In Jesus' name. Amen.

Charmaine Wamuyu   Kenya

Let's Talk:

1. What plan did God have for Esther?

2. Where can you read about God's plans for your life?

3. Why should you trust God's plans for you?

52. Taking a Stand

 Do you know what it means to stand for God? Esther's cousin, Mordecai, had to stand for God.

Esther was the new queen! Mordecai worked near the palace. One day he heard two men talking. They were making plans to kill the king. Mordecai told Queen Esther and she told the king. He had the two men killed. All of this was written in the king's record book.

Later the king gave a man named Haman an important job. The king ordered that everyone should honor Haman. They had to bow down to him. Mordecai would not bow down. He knew it would not please God. The other men asked Mordecai why he would not bow to Haman. He still took a stand for God.

 Taking a stand for God means to do what is right when others do wrong. It pleases God when you stand for Him. God will give you strength to do the right thing even when it is hard.

God gave Mordecai strength to take a stand and do what was right.

 You Can Pray:
Dear God, give me Your strength to stand for You. Help me do the right thing even when others are doing wrong. In Jesus' name. Amen.

Rose Schaefer   Age 8   Oregon

Let's Talk:

1. What does it mean to stand for God?
2. How did Mordecai stand for God?
3. What can you do when others want you to do wrong?

53. A New Law

 Do you remember what it means to stand for God? Mordecai stood for God. He would not bow to Haman. He did what was right.

Other people questioned Mordecai. He still refused to bow. They told Haman. Haman was angry. *What should I do about this man?* he wondered. He learned that Mordecai was a Jew. Then he knew just what to do.

God's Word Says:
" . . . he who stands firm to the end will be saved."
Matthew 10:22

Haman went to the king. He said, "There are some people who live in your kingdom. They do not obey your laws. Make a law that these people be killed." The king said, "Do what you want with these people."

Haman sent a letter to everyone in the kingdom. It told of this new law. The letter said that on a certain day the Persians should kill the Jews. What was Mordecai going to do? He had taken a stand for God. Now his people were in trouble.

Sometimes it is hard to stand for God. It may even cause you trouble. God knows what is best for you. Trust Him. Ask God for the strength you need to stand for Him.

 You Can Pray:
Dear God, I know I can trust You. You know what is best for me. Give me Your strength so I can stand for You. In Jesus' name. Amen.

Caitlyn S. See   Age 10   Pennsylvania

Let's Talk:

1. What did Mordecai do that made Haman angry?
2. What new law did Haman make?
3. What should you do when you need to stand for God?

54. God Gives Help

What do you do when something bad happens? Do you cry? Do you pray? Mordecai did both.

Mordecai heard that the Jews would be killed. He sat by the palace gate crying loudly. Esther sent a servant to ask why he was upset. The servant told her about the new law.

Mordecai wanted Esther to go to the king for help. The law said that no one could go to the king without being invited. Anyone who did could be killed. Esther sent a message to Mordecai that the king had not invited her.

Mordecai told Esther, "You are a Jew and may die too. Maybe God made you queen just for this." Esther asked Mordecai to bring the Jews together. They would not eat or drink for three days. They probably spent that time praying.

Then Esther went to the king. Seeing her made him happy. Esther invited the king and Haman to a big dinner. God had helped Esther.

When you have a problem, talk to God in prayer. He will hear and answer in the way that is best.

You Can Pray:
Dear God, thank You that I can talk to You in prayer. I know You hear and answer in the way that is best. In Jesus' name. Amen.

This Bible story can be found in Esther 4:1—5:4.

Jessie Castellanos Daisson   Age 8   Cuba

Let's Talk:

1. What did Mordecai want Esther to do?
2. How did God help Esther?
3. What should you do when you have a problem?

55. Haman's Pride

Do you ever brag? Haman did. He was at the queen's special dinner!

During the meal Esther invited the king and Haman to come to another dinner. Haman was happy! On his way home he passed Mordecai. Mordecai still refused to bow. This made Haman angry.

Haman bragged to his wife about having dinner with the king and queen. Then he told her about Mordecai. "Ask the king to kill him," Haman's wife said.

That night the king could not sleep. He asked his servant to read from his record book. The king read about how Mordecai had saved his life.

The next day the king asked Haman how he could honor someone. Haman thought the king was talking about him. He was very proud. Haman said, "Have the man wear your royal robe. Let him ride your horse." The king told Haman to do these things for Mordecai. Haman was no longer proud.

God does not want you to be proud. He wants you to be humble. Are you? Do you think of others before yourself? It pleases God when you are humble.

You Can Pray:
Dear God, I know You made me the way I am. Help me think of others. Help me be humble. In Jesus' name. Amen.

Jacob Mathews   Age 8   Oregon

Let's Talk:

1. How did Haman show he was proud?
2. What does it mean to be humble?
3. What are some things you might do if you are humble?

56. Victory for the Jews

 Do things always go the way you planned? Haman's plan sure had changed! He had to lead Mordecai through the city on the king's horse.

At the second dinner the king asked Esther what she wanted. He said he would give her anything. Esther said, "Please save my people! The Jews will be killed." The king asked who had made this law. Esther pointed to Haman.

The king was upset. He learned that Haman had planned to kill Mordecai. The king ordered that Haman be killed instead. Then he gave Mordecai Haman's old job.

Mordecai needed to do something to save the Jews. The king let him write a new law. It said the Jews could protect themselves. The Jewish people were happy! It was God's plan to use Esther and Mordecai to save them.

God is the ruler over everything. He loves you and controls what happens to you. Nothing is a surprise to Him. He has a plan to make things right in your life. Keep trusting God even when your plans do not work.

 You Can Pray:
Dear God, You are the ruler of all. Nothing surprises You. I trust You to work out the events in my life for my good. In Jesus' name. Amen.

This Bible story can be found in Esther 6:11—9:17.

Corina Clark   Age 7   Oregon

Let's Talk:

1. How did God use Esther to save the Jews?
2. How do you know that God was in control?
3. What should you do when your plans do not work?

115

57. Contest on Mt. Carmel

Is God most important in your life? God was not important to His people anymore. Could Elijah help them change?

God's people had a new king named Ahab. He did not love God. He wanted the people to worship an idol named Baal. This idol became more important than God to the people.

God's Word Says:
"You shall have no other gods before me."
Exodus 20:3

God sent a man named Elijah. He talked to the king. Elijah told the king to bring the people to Mount Carmel. God would show that He is the one true God. He alone should be worshipped.

At Mt. Carmel Elijah set up a contest. Two bulls would be killed. The leaders of Baal worship would pray to their idol. Elijah would pray to God. The true God would send fire to burn a bull. The people would see that the one true God should be most important to them.

God wants to be most important in your life. Do you spend all your time playing or watching TV? God wants you to take time to pray and read the Bible. Take time with God. It shows that He is important to you.

You Can Pray:
Dear God, I am sorry for not always putting You first. Help me remember that you are most important in my life. In Jesus' name. Amen.

Rachel Lacksman   Age 9   Namibia

Let's Talk:

1. Why did Elijah set up a contest on Mt. Carmel?
2. Who should be most important in your life?
3. What are some things that may be more important to you than God?

58. One True God

 Is there anything God cannot do? God's people needed to see that He could do anything. He is the one true God.

Elijah told the leaders of Baal worship, "Choose a bull. Kill it but do not set it on fire."

The leaders did this. They prayed for Baal to send fire. No fire came. "Shout louder," Elijah said. "Maybe he is busy or asleep." They prayed all day but nothing happened.

Next it was Elijah's turn. He put a bull on an altar of stones. "Pour four large jars of water over the bull," Elijah said. They did this three times. Water ran everywhere.

 Elijah prayed, "O Lord, send fire. Burn this bull so everyone will know that you are the one true God." Suddenly fire came from Heaven. It burned up the bull, the water and even the stones! The amazed people said, "The Lord—He is God!"

God proved He is the only true God. He can do anything. Maybe something hard is happening in your life. God can help you. He is powerful enough to do anything.

 You Can Pray:
Dear God, You are the one true God. You can do anything. Thank You for helping me with the hard things in my life. In Jesus' name. Amen.

Carina Martin   Age 7   Pennsylvania

Let's Talk:

1. How did God prove on Mt. Carmel that He is the one true God?
2. Is there anything too hard for God to do?
3. What hard thing do you need God to help you with?

59. Naboth's Vineyard

 Are you happy with what you have? Do you ever want what someone else has? King Ahab did.

King Ahab had a beautiful palace next to a vineyard. That is a garden where grapes are grown. The king wanted the vineyard. It belonged to a man named Naboth.

One day King Ahab said, "Naboth, let me have your vineyard. I will pay you for it." Naboth said, "No." The vineyard belonged to Naboth's family. He could not sell it. King Ahab felt sorry for himself. He lay on his bed and pouted.

Maybe you pout when you cannot have what you want. God wants you to be content. That means to be happy with what you have. Do not get angry and pout. Thank God for all the good things He has given you.

King Ahab was not content. "Cheer up," the queen said. "I will get you the vineyard." She had Naboth killed. Now King Ahab was happy. He could have the vineyard.

God was not happy with the king and queen. He punished them for what they had done to Naboth.

You Can Pray:

Dear God, thank You for all You have given me. I am sorry for not being content. Help me be happy with what I have. In Jesus' name. Amen.

La vigne de Naboth

Nice   Age 10   Cote d'Ivoire

Let's Talk:

1. Why did King Ahab pout?
2. What does it mean to be content?
3. What are some good things God has given you?

60. The Widow's Oil

 What are some of the things you need to live? A woman with many needs went to one of God's helpers, Elisha. Would he be able to help?

The woman's husband had died. She had two sons. "I do not have money to pay my bills," she said. If she did not pay the money, her sons would be taken away.

God's Word Says:
" . . . your Father knows what you need before you ask him."
Matthew 6:8

"What do you have in your house?" Elisha asked. "Only a jar of olive oil," she answered. Elisha told her to borrow many empty jars from her neighbors. He said to pour her oil into those jars and sell the oil.

The woman obeyed. She poured and poured oil into many jars. The oil did not run out until all the jars were full! She sold the oil. Then there was enough money to pay her bills. God had taken care of her needs.

Things are not always easy for God's children. Your family may have many needs. God knows and cares about you. He wants you to talk to Him about your needs. You can trust Him to care for you.

You Can Pray:
Dear God, thank You for caring about me. (Tell God about a need you have.) I trust You to take care of my needs. In Jesus' name. Amen.

This Bible story can be found in 2 Kings 4:1-7.

Kayla Goshern   Age 10   Colorado

Let's Talk:

1. What did the woman need?
2. What are some of your needs?
3. What can you do when you have a need?

61. Naaman

Do you tell others about God? That is being a witness. The Bible tells about a young girl that God used to be a witness.

Naaman was a leader in the Syrian army. He had a sickness called leprosy. Naaman's wife had a servant girl from Israel. The girl told Naaman's wife about God's helper. His name was Elisha. She knew Elisha could help Naaman.

God's Word Says:
"You are my witnesses, . . . and my servant whom I have chosen. . . ."
Isaiah 43:10

The servant girl was being a witness. She told about God's helper. God wants you to witness too. Being a witness means to tell others what God has done for you. Tell them why Jesus died on the cross. Tell how they can have their sins forgiven. You can be a witness just like the servant girl.

Naaman's wife told him what the girl said. Naaman went to Elisha's house. A servant told Naaman to go and dip seven times in the Jordan River. Then he would be healed.

Naaman was angry but he finally obeyed. He went to the Jordan River and dipped down seven times. Naaman was healed! God had made him well.

You Can Pray:
Dear God, thank You for forgiving my sin. Help me tell others how they can be forgiven. In Jesus' name. Amen.

This Bible story can be found in 2 Kings 5:1-15.

Megan Moran   Age 5   Japan

Let's Talk:

1. What did the servant girl tell Naaman's wife?
2. What does it mean to witness for God?
3. Who can you tell about Jesus this week?

62. Daniel's Test

Is it always easy to do what is right? A young man named Daniel wanted to do right. He needed God's help.

An enemy king sent soldiers to fight God's people. These soldiers took a group of young men back to serve the king. Daniel and three of his friends were part of this group.

They were taken to the palace. They were given food from the king's table. Daniel knew God would not want them to eat this food. God gave Daniel courage. He asked the servant to let them eat only vegetables and drink only water for ten days.

God helped Daniel and his friends. At the end of the ten-day test they looked stronger than all the other young men. God had blessed Daniel and his friends because they did what was right.

God wants you to do what is right. Maybe you want to go with your friends or play on the computer. You know you should study. Ask God to help you choose to do the right thing. God will give you power to do what is right.

You Can Pray:
Dear God, sometimes it is hard for me to do the right thing. Please give me strength to do what is right. In Jesus' name. Amen.

This Bible story can be found in Daniel 1:1-21.

Kayla Brown   Age 8   Ohio

Let's Talk:
1. What did God give Daniel courage to do?
2. What happened after Daniel's ten-day test?
3. When do you need God's help to do what is right?

63. The Fiery Furnace

 Would you obey God even if it caused you trouble? That is what happened to Daniel's three friends.

The king gave an order. "Everyone must bow and worship my statue. Those who do not will be thrown into a flaming furnace." Daniel's friends refused to bow to the statue. They obeyed God.

God's Word Says:

" . . . I will keep your law and obey it with all my heart."
Psalm 119:34

The king was angry! Daniel's friends told the king, "We will not bow. Our God is able to save us. Even if He does not, we will not worship the statue."

Daniel's friends knew they could get into trouble. Still they obeyed God. Obeying God may cause you trouble. Others may tease or hurt you. God can give you courage to obey Him anyway. That is what He did for Daniel's friends.

"Make the fire seven times hotter!" the king said. "Throw them in." The young men were thrown into the hot furnace. Then the king saw them walking around inside. Another man was with them. The king called Daniel's friends out. They were not burned.

The king praised God. God had sent His angel to rescue Daniel's friends.

 You Can Pray:

Dear God, please give me courage to obey You even if it causes me trouble. Thank You for always being with me. In Jesus' name. Amen.

Frederik Lipcei   Age 9   Slovakia

Let's Talk:

1. Why did Daniel's friends refuse to bow down to the statue?
2. What happened to them because they would not bow down?
3. When do you need to ask God for courage to obey Him?

64. The Lion's Den

 Do you ever get tired of doing what is right? God wants you to be faithful to Him. Was Daniel faithful?

Daniel prayed to God every day. The king liked Daniel and made him a leader. The other leaders were jealous. They looked for bad things Daniel did. They could not find any.

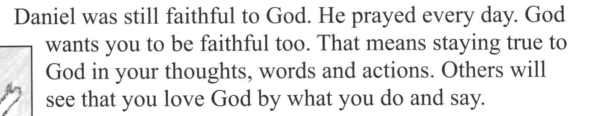

God's Word Says:
"A faithful man will be richly blessed. . . ."
Proverbs 28:20

The men said to the king, "Make a law that people cannot pray to any god but you. If they do, throw them to the lions." The king agreed.

Daniel was still faithful to God. He prayed every day. God wants you to be faithful too. That means staying true to God in your thoughts, words and actions. Others will see that you love God by what you do and say.

Daniel was faithful to pray to God. The king was sad when the men told him. The law could not be changed. Daniel was thrown to the lions.

The next morning the king went to the lions' den. He asked, "Did your God save you, Daniel?"

"Yes," Daniel answered. "God sent an angel to close the lions' mouths."

You Can Pray:
Dear God, thank You for everything You have done for me. Please help me be faithful to You. In Jesus' name. Amen.

This Bible story can be found in Daniel 6:1-28.

Roberto Zapata Rodriguez   Age 10   Cuba

Let's Talk:
1. How was Daniel faithful to God?
2. What does it mean to be faithful?
3. How can you be faithful to God?

65. Jonah Runs Away

What if God told you to do something you did not want to do? God had a job for a man named Jonah. Jonah did not want to do it.

The people who lived in the city of Nineveh were very sinful. God told Jonah, "Go to Nineveh. Tell the people they have sinned. Tell them I will punish them."

God's Word Says:
" . . . be careful to obey so that it may go well with you. . . ."
Deuteronomy 6:3

Jonah tried to run from God. He did not go to Nineveh. He got on a ship that was going the other way. God sent a big storm to stop Jonah.

It is important to obey God. What does God say you should do? Be kind. Obey your parents. Tell the truth. God tells you many other things in the Bible. Are you careful to obey God? Jonah did not obey. God had to send a big storm.

Jonah told the sailors the storm was his fault. "Throw me into the sea," he said. The men did what Jonah said and the storm stopped. A big fish came and swallowed Jonah. Now what would happen to him?

You Can Pray:
Dear God, I love You and want to obey Your Word. Please help me do what You say. In Jesus' name. Amen.

This Bible story can be found in Jonah 1:1-17.

Avery Simmons   Age 6   Virginia

Let's Talk:
1. What did Jonah do when God told him to go to Nineveh?
2. What are some things God tells you to do in the Bible?
3. What should you do when you do not want to obey God?

66. Jonah Obeys God

What should you say when you do something bad? Do you say you are sorry? Was Jonah ready to say he was sorry?

A big fish had swallowed Jonah. He spent three days inside the fish. Jonah confessed his sin to God. He told God he was sorry he had not obeyed.

God wants people who know Him to confess their sins to Him. Are there sins you should talk to God about? Tell Him what you did wrong. Agree that it is sin. Say you are sorry. Ask God to help you do what is right. He will hear your prayer and forgive you.

God heard Jonah's prayer. The fish spit Jonah out on land. Again God told Jonah to go to Nineveh. This time Jonah obeyed. He told the people, "You have sinned against God. He will destroy the city in 40 days."

The people believed God. The king said, "Pray to God. Maybe He will not punish us." God heard the people's prayers. He knew they were sorry. God told Jonah that He would not punish the people. God forgave them.

You Can Pray:
Dear God, I know it makes You sad when I sin. I am sorry. Remind me to confess my sins to You. In Jesus' name. Amen.

Nathaniel Forst   Age 6   Quebec, Canada

Let's Talk:

1. What did Jonah do while he was in the big fish?
2. What does it mean to confess your sins to God?
3. What sins do you need to confess to God right now?

67. God Sends His Son

 Have you ever had to wait a long time for a promise to be kept? God was about to keep a promise He had made a long time ago.

God had promised to send someone to save His people from sin. Now was the time for that Savior to come.

God sent the angel Gabriel to a young woman named Mary. Gabriel said, "God has chosen you to have a special baby. He will be God's Son."

God's Word Says:
" . . . the Father has sent his Son to be the Savior of the world."
1 John 4:14

Mary answered, "How can this happen?" Gabriel told her that anything is possible with God.

Mary was engaged to a man named Joseph. He found out that Mary was going to have a baby. An angel told Joseph that Mary's baby was from God. The angel said, "Name the baby Jesus. He will save His people from their sin." Jesus would be the Savior God had promised.

This promise is for you too. What if God had not kept His promise? Your sins would not be forgiven. You would not be God's child. Have you thanked God for keeping His promise by sending His Son?

You Can Pray:
Dear God, thank You for keeping Your promise to send a Savior. Thank You for forgiving my sin. In Jesus' name. Amen.

This Bible story can be found in Matthew 1:18-24; Luke 1:26-38.

Rachel Vile   Age 9   Illinois

Let's Talk:

1. What promise had God made to His people long ago?
2. Why did God send His Son into the world?
3. Why are you thankful that God sent His Son?

68. Jesus Is Born

 Have you ever had to go and live in a different place? Were you scared? That is what happened to Mary and Joseph.

The leaders were counting all the people in the country. Each family had to go to the town their family came from. Joseph and Mary went to Bethlehem. The trip was hard. Mary would have her baby soon.

God's Word Says:
"Trust in the LORD with all your heart and lean not on your own understanding."
Proverbs 3:5

Mary and Joseph looked for a place to stay. All the rooms were full. They had to stay in a stable where animals were kept. This was not a good place for a baby to be born. Still Mary and Joseph trusted God.

Trusting God means to believe that He will take care of you. Maybe you have to move to a different place. Are you scared or lonely? God is always with you. He knows where you are. You can trust Him to take care of you.

God took care of Mary and Joseph. God's Son was born in the stable. Mary and Joseph named Him Jesus. Mary wrapped Jesus in cloth. She made a bed for Him in a manger.

You Can Pray:
Dear God, thank You for always being with me. Help me trust You to take care of me all the time. In Jesus' name. Amen.

Kelsey Ebersole   Age 10   Pennsylvania

Let's Talk:

1. Where did Mary and Joseph have to stay in Bethlehem?
2. What does it mean to trust God?
3. What should you remember when you are scared or lonely?

69. Shepherds and Angels

 What do you do when you hear good news? Do you want to tell everyone? That is what some shepherds did.

The night Jesus was born shepherds were in a field taking care of their sheep. Suddenly an angel came down in bright, shining light. The shepherds were afraid.

God's Word Says:
". . . Go into all the world and preach the good news to all creation."
Mark 16:15

"Do not be afraid. I have good news!" the angel said. "A Savior has been born. You will find Him in Bethlehem. He is lying in a manger."

Suddenly many other angels came from Heaven. They praised God. "Glory to God in the highest. Peace on Earth to everyone." Then the angels left.

"Let us go to Bethlehem," the shepherds said. "Let us see if we can find this baby."

 The shepherds rushed to Bethlehem. They found the baby just like the angels said. They hurried away to tell others this good news.

God wants you to tell others about Jesus. Tell them that Jesus came to save them from their sins. He died for their sins on a cross. He came back to life again! All who believe in Jesus will have eternal life.

You Can Pray:
Dear God, thank You for sending Jesus to save the world from sin. Help me tell others this good news. In Jesus' name. Amen.

This Bible story can be found in Luke 2:8-20.

Emily Nussbaum   Age 9   Alberta, Canada

Let's Talk:

1. What good news did the angels tell the shepherds?
2. What good news about Jesus does God want you to tell others?
3. Who can you tell this good news?

70. The Wise Men

Can a star lead people to Jesus? Long ago a special star led some wise men to Jesus so they could worship Him.

The night Jesus was born a new star appeared. Wise men who lived far away saw it. They knew it meant a new King was born. They followed the star to find the baby.

The star led them to Jerusalem. The men asked about this new King. King Herod was worried. He thought this new King would take his place.

God's Word Says:
"Come, let us bow down in worship. . . ."
Psalm 95:6

"Go to Bethlehem," Herod said. "When you find this King, come and tell me so I can worship Him." That was not true. Herod really wanted Him killed.

The star was above Mary and Joseph's house in Bethlehem. The men went in and saw Jesus. They gave Him gifts. They bowed in worship.

Jesus is God the Son. He is the King over all kings. He should be worshiped. You worship by praising someone. You can praise Jesus in song and in prayer. You also praise Him by obeying.

God told the wise men in a dream not to return to Herod.

You Can Pray:
Dear God, You are the King of all kings. You are the one who made the stars. You love me and care for me. Thank You! In Jesus' name. Amen.

142

Alyssa Hatteberg   Age 9   Ohio

Let's Talk:

1. Why did the wise men follow the star?
2. Why should you worship Jesus?
3. What are some ways you can worship Jesus?

71. Jesus as a Boy

 How can you show God that you love Him? When Jesus was a child, He showed the answer to this question.

Jesus lived with His family in Nazareth. Mary and Joseph took Him to Jerusalem when He was 12. They went to the temple. They would worship God.

God's Word Says:
"Whoever has my commands [the Bible] and obeys them . . . loves me. . . ."
John 14:21

Soon it was time to go home. Mary and Joseph thought Jesus was walking with His friends. That night they looked for Jesus. They could not find Him. They hurried back to Jerusalem.

 Finally Mary and Joseph found Jesus at the temple. He was talking to the teachers about God. Everyone was surprised at how much Jesus knew.

Mary told Jesus they had been worried. They had been looking for Him for three days. "Didn't you know I would be in my Father's house?" Jesus asked. He knew God was His Father.

Jesus went home with Mary and Joseph. He obeyed them. God wants you to obey like Jesus did. You obey God by obeying your parents. You show God you love Him by obeying the Bible.

You Can Pray:
Dear God, I want to be like Jesus. Please help me show that I love You by obeying. In Jesus' name. Amen.

This Bible story can be found in Luke 2:41-52.

Kali Saint Age 5 California

Let's Talk:
1. What was Jesus doing in the temple?
2. What are some ways you should obey God?
3. What are you showing God when you obey Him?

72. Jesus Is Tempted

Who is God's enemy? It is Satan. He wants people to sin. Satan wanted Jesus to sin too.

Jesus had become an adult. He was in the desert for 40 days. He did not eat. He prayed to God. Then Satan came and said, "If you are God's Son, turn these stones into bread."

Jesus answered, "It is written [in the Bible] that people need more than food to live. They need the Word of God."

Satan took Jesus to the top of the temple. He told Jesus to jump off to prove He is God's Son. Jesus told Satan, "It is written that you should not test God."

Next Satan took Jesus to a mountain. "Look around," Satan said. "I will give all this to you if you worship me."

"Go away, Satan!" Jesus answered. "It is written that only God should be worshipped." Satan left Him.

Jesus used Bible verses to fight Satan. You can use Bible verses to help you keep from sinning. Keep God's Word in your heart by learning verses. Remembering these verses will help you say no to sin.

You Can Pray:
Dear God, thank You for the Bible! Help me use Your Word so I will not sin. In Jesus' name. Amen.

Samantha Jo Groenke   Age 8   Missouri

Let's Talk:

1. What was one thing Satan wanted Jesus to do?
2. What did Jesus use to fight Satan?
3. What can help you say no to sin?

73. Jesus Chooses Disciples

 Have you ever played follow the leader? You have to do what the leader does. Jesus is looking for people to follow Him.

Jesus knew that someday He was going back to Heaven. He wanted to choose people He could teach about God. They could tell other people about God when Jesus was gone.

God's Word Says:
" . . . you should follow in his [Jesus'] steps."
1 Peter 2:21

One day Jesus was walking by the sea. Peter and Andrew were fishing. "Come, follow Me," Jesus said. They obeyed. Then Jesus saw James and John by their boats. They followed Jesus too.

God wants you to follow Jesus. If you are His child, you will try to be like Him. How do you know what Jesus is like? You can read about Him in the Bible and in this book. You can pray. Ask God to make you more like Jesus. It pleases God when you follow Jesus.

There were other people who followed Jesus too. He chose 12 of them to be His disciples. Their names were Simon Peter, Andrew, James, John, Philip, Bartholomew, Matthew, Thomas, James, Simon, Thaddaeus and Judas.

Are you a friend and follower of Jesus?

 You Can Pray:
Dear God, I want to be like Jesus. Please help me follow Him in all I do and say. In Jesus' name. Amen.

This Bible story can be found in Matthew 10:2-4; Mark 1:16-20.

Madison Gober   Age 8   Pennsylvania

Let's Talk:

1. Why did Jesus choose 12 men to follow Him?

2. Can you name three of Jesus' followers?

3. How can you follow Jesus?

149

74. Jesus Calms a Storm

Does it scare you when a storm comes? Jesus' disciples were in a storm one night. They were afraid!

Jesus sat by the lake teaching the people all day. He was tired. Jesus said to His disciples, "Let us go to the other side of the lake."

God's Word Says:
"So do not fear, for I am with you. . . ."
Isaiah 41:10

They got into a boat and started across the lake. Jesus fell asleep. Suddenly there was a big storm. The wind blew. Waves crashed! Water splashed inside the boat.

"Wake up, Jesus! Don't you care if we drown?" the disciples said. They were afraid!

What makes you afraid? If you are God's child, Jesus is always with you. Ask Him to give you His peace. He can make you calm when you are afraid. Jesus has power to help you get through anything.

Jesus could help the disciples. "Peace. Be still!" He said to the wind and the waves. At once the lake was calm. Jesus looked at His disciples. "Why are you afraid?" He asked. He wanted the disciples to trust Him.

The disciples were amazed. "Even the wind and waves obey Him!" they said.

You Can Pray:
Dear God, thank You for always being with me. Remind me to ask for Your peace when I am afraid. In Jesus' name. Amen.

This Bible story can be found in Mark 4:35-41.

Eddy David Gonzalez Palacio   Age 8   Cuba

Let's Talk:

1. Why were the disciples afraid?
2. What does it mean to have God's peace?
3. What should you do when you are afraid?

75. Jairus's Daughter

Do parents worry when their children get sick? The Bible tells about a father named Jairus. He was very worried about his sick daughter.

Jairus came and fell at Jesus' feet. "My only daughter is sick," he said. "She may die. Please come and make her well."

God's Word Says:
"And without faith it is impossible to please God. . . ."
Hebrews 11:6

Jesus went with Jairus to help the girl. A man came to Jairus with a message. "Do not bother Jesus any more," he said. "Your daughter has died."

"Do not be afraid," Jesus told Jairus. "Have faith and your daughter will be healed." Jairus needed to believe that Jesus could still help his daughter.

God wants you to believe that He can help you. Believing that God will do what He says is called *faith*. When you have a problem, have faith in God. He has power to help you.

Jairus had faith that Jesus could help. When they came to the house, Jesus went inside. He took Jairus's daughter by the hand. "Get up," He said. The girl stood right up. She was alive! Her parents were amazed at Jesus' power.

You Can Pray:
Dear God, I believe You have power to help me. (Tell God about your problem.) Thank You for helping me. In Jesus' name. Amen.

Molly Kitchen   Age 6   Florida

Let's Talk:

1. Why did Jairus come to Jesus?
2. What is faith?
3. What problem can God help you with today?

76. Feeding the 5,000

Is it hard to share? You may not think you have much to share. But God can use even a little bit to help others!

A crowd of more than 5,000 people listened to Jesus teach all day. They were far from their homes. It was late. The people were hungry.

Jesus asked His disciples, "Where should we get bread for the people to eat?" Jesus knew what He was going to do. He wanted His disciples to trust Him.

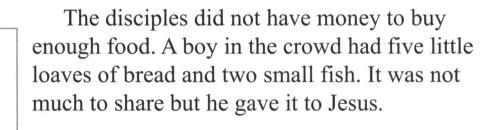

The disciples did not have money to buy enough food. A boy in the crowd had five little loaves of bread and two small fish. It was not much to share but he gave it to Jesus.

What can you share? You can share a smile with a sad friend. You can share kind words with others. You can share your time to help someone with a problem. Let God use what you have to help others.

Jesus took the boy's lunch. He thanked God for it. The disciples fed all the people. Everyone had all they could eat. There was even food left over!

You Can Pray:
Dear God, help me share what I have. Thank You for using it to help someone else. In Jesus' name. Amen.

Emily Buschman   Age 7   Colorado

Let's Talk:

1. What did the boy give to Jesus?
2. What can you share for God to use?
3. How can Jesus use what you have to help others?

77. The Good Samaritan

 How do you show love? Saying kind words shows love. Doing nice things shows love. Sometimes the best way to show love is to help someone.

One day Jesus told this story to teach about loving other people.

God's Word Says:
". . . Love your neighbor as yourself."
Luke 10:27

A man took a long trip. Robbers beat him and took his clothes. They left him to die. Three men walked by. The first two men were supposed to be God's helpers. They did not stop to help the man. They walked away.

The third man was from an enemy country. He stopped and showed God's love. He bandaged the man's wounds. He paid for a place for the man to stay. The man was able to rest and get well.

Jesus told this story so people would know they should show love to everyone.

God wants you to show His love too. You can do extra things at home without being asked. You can help a friend with his or her schoolwork. You can be kind to an older person. These are some ways God's children can show His love to others.

You Can Pray:
Dear God, thank You for loving me. Help me show Your love to others every day. In Jesus' name. Amen.

This Bible story can be found in Luke 10:25-37.

Etonam Ameobe   Age 9   Ghana

Let's Talk:
1. How did the man in Jesus' story show love?
2. Who are some people you can show God's love to?
3. How can you show God's love today?

157

78. The Ten Lepers

 Do you remember to say thank you? It is important to thank people for the nice things they do. It is even more important to thank God!

One day Jesus saw ten sick men. They had leprosy. It was a terrible disease. No medicine could cure it. The men had to live away from other people. It was a very sad life.

"Jesus, have pity on us!" the men called out. They wanted Jesus to heal them.

 Jesus cared about these men. He said, "Go show yourselves to the temple leaders." Only the leaders could say if the men were really well.

The men trusted Jesus. They left to see the temple leaders. As they went, they were healed. The leprosy was gone! Jesus had healed all ten men. Only one of them came back to thank Him.

Do you remember to thank God? Think of all He does for you. He gives you air to breathe. He has given you a family and friends to love. Have you stopped to thank Him? Thanking God is always the right thing to do!

 You Can Pray:
Dear God, there is so much to thank You for. (Tell God some things you are thankful for.) Remind me to be thankful every day. In Jesus' name. Amen.

Kristin Fisler   Age 7   Pennsylvania

Let's Talk:

1. What did Jesus do for the ten men?
2. Why do you think only one man came back to thank Jesus?
3. What are some things you can thank God for?

79. Jesus and the Children

 Do you ever feel too young? There are some things you cannot do if you are little. Coming to Jesus is something you can do even if you are young.

Many people wanted to be around Jesus. He was always very busy. One day parents brought their children to Jesus. They knew Jesus was special. He was God the Son. They wanted Jesus to bless their children.

God's Word Says:
Jesus said, "Let the little children come to me. . . ."
Mark 10:14

 Jesus' disciples scolded the people. They told them to keep their children away. The disciples thought Jesus had more important things to do.

Jesus saw what the disciples did. He was angry! Jesus said, "Let the children come to Me. Do not keep them away!"

Jesus loved the children. He loves you. You can talk to Him anytime. He is never too busy for you. You are never in His way. He wants you to spend time with Him. He wants you to tell Him what is happening in your life. Other people may not have time for you. Jesus always does!

Jesus took the children in His arms and blessed them.

You Can Pray:
Dear God, thank You for loving me so much. I am glad I can talk to You anytime. In Jesus' name. Amen.

Lina Asante   Age 8   Ghana

Let's Talk:

1. Why were parents bringing their children to Jesus?
2. Why was Jesus angry?
3. What are some things you can talk to Jesus about?

80. Blind Bartimaeus

 Have you ever praised someone? That means to say something good about him or her. God deserves your praise most of all!

Jesus and His disciples were leaving Jericho. A large crowd followed. They probably made a lot of noise. One voice was heard above all the noise.

God's Word Says:
"I will praise you, O LORD, with all my heart. . . ."
Psalm 9:1

"Jesus," a man called. "Help me!" It was a blind man named Bartimaeus. He could not see but he knew Jesus was coming. The people told Bartimaeus to be quiet. Instead he shouted louder.

 Jesus stopped. "What do you want me to do for you?" He asked Bartimaeus. "I want to see!" Bartimaeus said. "Go," said Jesus. "Your faith has healed you."

Right away Bartimaeus could see! He could see the crowd. He could see the tall trees. Best of all, he could see Jesus! Bartimaeus began to follow Jesus. He and all the people praised God.

God deserves to be praised. Every day He does wonderful things! He loves you. He takes care of you. He gives you everything you need. You can praise God for who He is and what He does.

You Can Pray:
Dear God, I praise You for being so good. Thank You for all You do for me. In Jesus' name. Amen.

Carly DeBurgh   Age 9   Wisconsin

Let's Talk:

1. Why was Bartimaeus calling to Jesus?
2. Why did the crowd praise God?
3. What can you praise God for?

81. Zacchaeus

Have you ever cheated? Cheating is not playing fair. It is doing something wrong to help yourself. One day Jesus met a man who liked to cheat.

The man was a tax collector named Zacchaeus. He took extra money for himself. He was cheating and stealing.

God's Word Says:
". . . if anyone is in Christ, he is a new creation. . . ."
2 Corinthians 5:17

One day Jesus was walking through Jericho. All the people came to see Him. Zacchaeus was too short to see. He climbed up a tree to watch Jesus coming. Soon Jesus stopped in front of him.

"Zacchaeus, come down!" Jesus said. "I am going to your house today!" The people grumbled. Why would Jesus go to Zacchaeus's house?

After Zacchaeus believed in Jesus, he was changed. "I will give money to the poor," Zacchaeus said. "I will pay back anyone I have cheated!" He was changed on the inside!

Jesus wants to change you on the inside. He wants to help you say no to sin and obey God. He can help you stop cheating and do what is right. He can help you stop lying and tell the truth. You will be different if Jesus lives in you.

You Can Pray:

Dear God, thank You for saving me from my sin. Change me from the inside out. Then others will know You live in me. In Jesus' name. Amen.

This Bible story can be found in Luke 19:1-10.

Hillary Charles   Age 6   Kenya

Let's Talk:

1. What made Zacchaeus want to stop cheating?
2. How has Jesus changed your life?
3. Are there other changes you need Him to make?

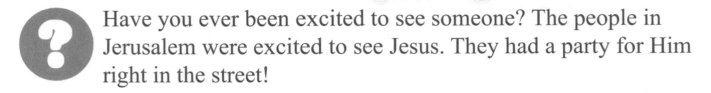

? Have you ever been excited to see someone? The people in Jerusalem were excited to see Jesus. They had a party for Him right in the street!

Jesus and His disciples were walking toward the city. He told two of the disciples to get a donkey and its colt. The disciples put their coats on the donkeys. Jesus sat on the coats. He rode toward the city. Long ago God had said this would happen. The Savior would come into Jerusalem riding a donkey!

God's Word Says:
"Great is the LORD and most worthy of praise. . . ."
Psalm 145:3

The people were excited to see Jesus. They cut palm branches and laid them on the road. Some people spread their coats on the road as Jesus came into the city.

"Hosanna! Blessed is He who comes in the name of the Lord!" The people shouted for joy. Jesus had done great things. He was worthy of their praise.

God is also worthy of your praise. Tell Him how wonderful He is. You can praise God when you are by yourself. You can praise Him when you are with other people. Have you praised God today?

You Can Pray:
Dear God, You are a great God. You deserve my praise! Remind me to praise You every day. In Jesus' name. Amen.

Sara Dellinger   Age 8   Colorado

Let's Talk:

1. How did the people praise Jesus?
2. How can you praise Jesus?
3. When should you praise Jesus?

83. Jesus Washes Feet

 Do you like to walk barefoot? Bare feet get very dirty. One night Jesus used dirty feet to teach His disciples a special lesson.

Jesus and His disciples were sharing a meal. It was the last meal Jesus would eat before dying on the cross.

Jesus got up from the table. He took water and a towel. He washed His disciples' dirty feet. In most Jewish homes a servant would do this job. Jesus was willing to serve His disciples.

God's Word Says:
" . . . serve one another in love."
Galatians 5:13

 Jesus finished washing the disciples' feet. "Do you understand why I did this?" He asked. "I have washed your feet. Do the same thing for each other." Jesus was telling His disciples to serve each other like He had served them.

You need to serve others like Jesus did. You can serve a younger child. You can help with something he or she cannot do. You can serve your family by helping around the house. You can serve your teacher by cleaning up the classroom. When you serve others, you are serving God.

Jesus wanted His disciples to learn to serve others.

You Can Pray:
Dear God, thank You that I can serve others. Help me serve like Jesus did. In Jesus' name. Amen.

This Bible story can be found in John 13:1-17.

Maximilian Klinkert   Age 9   Germany

Let's Talk:
1. Why did Jesus wash His disciples' feet?
2. Why should you serve other people?
3. What are some ways you can serve?

84. Jesus Is Betrayed

 Have you ever felt betrayed? Betraying someone is turning against him or her. It is when a friend acts like an enemy. Jesus had a friend like that!

Jesus and His disciples were sharing their last meal. Soon He was going to die on the cross. Jesus said, "One of you will betray me." The disciples were surprised. Who would betray Jesus? Jesus knew it would be Judas.

God's Word Says:
"So do not be ashamed to testify [tell or show] about our Lord [Jesus]. . . ."
2 Timothy 1:8

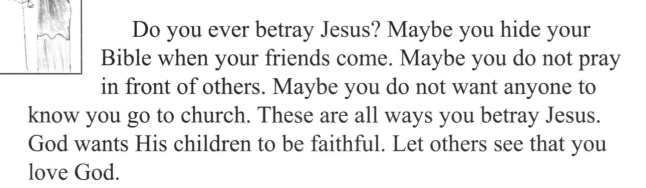 Judas left the meal. He told Jesus' enemies where to find Jesus. The men paid Judas 30 silver coins. He had pretended to be a friend of Jesus. Now Judas betrayed Him. He hurt Jesus by helping His enemies.

Do you ever betray Jesus? Maybe you hide your Bible when your friends come. Maybe you do not pray in front of others. Maybe you do not want anyone to know you go to church. These are all ways you betray Jesus. God wants His children to be faithful. Let others see that you love God.

Judas was not faithful to Jesus. Later that night he brought Jesus' enemies to Him. They arrested Jesus and took Him away.

You Can Pray:
Dear God, I do not want to betray You. Help me to be faithful and show others that I love You. In Jesus' name. Amen.

Giovanna Munoz Galvav   Age 9   Brazil

Let's Talk:

1. How did Judas betray Jesus?

2. What are some ways people betray Jesus today?

3. How can you show that you are faithful to Jesus?

85. Jesus Suffers

Have you ever seen a trial? A judge decides if a person is guilty. Jesus was put on trial. He was not guilty of anything wrong!

Jesus was arrested. He was taken from one temple leader to another. They wanted Jesus to die because He said He was God's Son.

They sent Jesus to a government leader named Pilate. He knew Jesus was not guilty. He wanted to set Jesus free. The people shouted, "No!" Pilate wanted to make the people happy. He had the soldiers beat Jesus. They made Him wear a crown of thorns. They slapped His face and said mean things.

> **God's Word Says:**
> " . . . Christ suffered for you. . . ."
> 1 Peter 2:21

Jesus is God the Son. Why did He have to suffer so much? He was willing to suffer and die for your sin. If you have trusted in Jesus, you are God's child. Your sin is forgiven. Have you thanked Jesus? You should thank Him every day. He went through so much for you.

Jesus suffered but the people still were not happy. They wanted Jesus to die. Pilate told the soldiers to nail Jesus to a cross.

You Can Pray:

Dear God, Jesus did not deserve to be punished. Thank You that He was willing to suffer for me. In Jesus' name. Amen.

This Bible story can be found in John 18:13-14, 28—19:16.

Allison Petrov   Age 8   Missouri

Let's Talk:

1. Why did the temple leaders want Jesus to die?
2. What are some ways Jesus suffered?
3. How can you show you are thankful for all Jesus has done?

86. Jesus Dies

 How do you know God loves you? Jesus proved it. He did something for you that no one else would do.

Pilate sent Jesus to die. Soldiers made Jesus carry His cross up a hill. They pounded nails into His hands and feet. He was hung on the cross. Blood came from His body.

All this was God's plan. He proved His love by sending His Son. Jesus died for you. He could have stopped the soldiers. He was willing to bleed and die so your sin could be forgiven.

 Have your sins been forgiven? The Bible says, " . . . Believe in the Lord Jesus, and you will be saved . . ." (Acts 16:31). Agree with God that you have sinned. Trust that Jesus took your punishment. He will forgive your sin. You will be saved. You will not have to be kept away from God. That is why Jesus came to Earth.

Jesus hung on the cross for a long time. Then the sky grew dark. Jesus cried out, "It is finished!" He had paid for your sin. He bowed His head and died.

You Can Pray:
Dear God, I am sorry I have sinned. I believe Jesus died to save me from my sin. Please forgive me! Thank You for loving me. In Jesus' name. Amen.

174

This Bible story can be found in Luke 23:26-46; John 19:28-30.

Mary Hargrove   Age 6   California

Let's Talk:

1. How do you know God loves you?
2. How did Jesus die?
3. What do you need to do to be saved?

87. Jesus Is Buried

 Has someone you know died? You feel sad when someone close to you dies. Jesus' friends were very sad when He died.

Jesus had hung on the cross for a long time. After He died, a soldier near the cross said, "This was the Son of God!"

It is true. Jesus is the Son of God! You can thank God for sending Jesus. Thank Him that Jesus was willing to die and save you from sin. Thank God that Jesus took your punishment. Thank Him for forgiving your sin.

After Jesus died, His friends wrapped His body in cloth. They carried it to a garden. They gently placed His body in a tomb that was like a cave.

A big stone was rolled in front so no one could go in or out. Guards stood by the tomb. They made sure no one could take Jesus' body away.

Jesus' friends were very sad and afraid. They thought they might be arrested because they had been with Jesus. They did not understand that Jesus had to die for their sins.

You Can Pray:
Dear God, thank You for sending Jesus to die for my sin. Thank You for forgiving me and saving me. In Jesus' name. Amen.

Jennifer Adusei   Age 9   Ghana

Let's Talk:

1. What did Jesus' friends do with His body?
2. Why were Jesus' friends afraid after He died?
3. Why should you be thankful that Jesus died?

88. Jesus Comes Alive

Do you like surprises? It is exciting when something good happens that you do not expect. A lady named Mary was about to have a wonderful surprise!

Three days after Jesus died, Mary came to the tomb. She saw that the big stone had been rolled away. Jesus' body was not there.

Mary ran and told Peter and John, two of Jesus' disciples. They ran to the tomb. They found only the cloth Jesus' body had been wrapped in. They did not understand what had happened to Jesus.

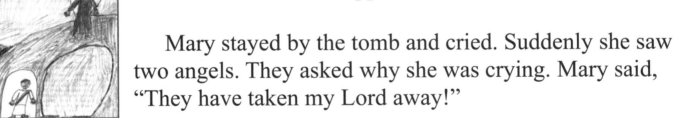

Mary stayed by the tomb and cried. Suddenly she saw two angels. They asked why she was crying. Mary said, "They have taken my Lord away!"

Mary turned and saw a man. He asked, "Who are you looking for?"

Mary did not know the man was Jesus. Then He said her name. Mary was so surprised and happy! She ran back to tell the disciples, "Jesus is alive!"

Who can you tell that Jesus is alive? Tell your friends and family. They need to know Jesus died for their sins and came back to life.

You Can Pray:
Dear God, I know Jesus is alive. Help me tell others what Jesus did for them. In Jesus' name. Amen.

This Bible story can be found in John 20:1-18.

Jordan D. Knight   Age 10   Pennsylvania

Let's Talk:

1. What did Mary find when she went to the tomb?
2. What did Mary do after she talked to Jesus?
3. Who can you tell about Jesus this week?

179

89. Jesus Appears

Do you know what doubt is? It is when you do not believe something is true. Some people in the Bible doubted that Jesus was alive.

Jesus' disciples were in a room with the doors locked. Suddenly Jesus stood in the room with them! They saw the nail marks in His hands. It was really Jesus. They were excited! He was alive!

God's Word Says:
" . . .blessed [happy] are those who have not seen [Jesus] and yet have believed."
John 20:29

A disciple named Thomas was not there. The other disciples told him Jesus was alive. Thomas said, "I will not believe unless I see Him." He doubted that it was true.

Are there times you doubt God? Do you really believe God loves and cares for you? Do you believe He is always there to help you? You can trust everything God says in His Word. You do not ever have to doubt God.

Thomas doubted. Later he was with the other disciples. Suddenly Jesus stood in the room with them. He told Thomas to stop doubting and believe. Thomas said to Him, "My Lord and my God!" Thomas saw Jesus for himself. Then he believed and did not doubt.

You Can Pray:
Dear God, thank You that the Bible is true. Help me believe Your Word and not doubt. In Jesus' name. Amen.

Sarah Mayers   Age 5   Florida

Let's Talk:

1. How did the disciples know it was Jesus in the room with them?
2. Why did Thomas doubt that Jesus was alive?
3. What are some things God wants you to believe about Him?

90. Return to Heaven

? Are you ever afraid to tell people about Jesus? There is someone who can give you courage to witness. Jesus' friends found out about Him.

Jesus had come back to life. He stayed on Earth 40 more days. Jesus told His friends something that was going to happen. "The Holy Spirit will give you power to witness," He said. "You must tell people everywhere about Me." God the Holy Spirit would give them courage to tell others about Jesus.

> **God's Word Says:**
> ". . . you will be my witnesses. . . ."
> Acts 1:8

If you have believed in Jesus, the Holy Spirit lives in you. He will give you courage to witness. Pray when you are afraid. Ask God to help you. Ask Him for the right words to tell about Jesus. Ask Him to help you be brave.

Jesus was finished talking to His friends. As they watched, He went up into the sky. A cloud hid Jesus so they could not see Him.

Two angels stood beside Jesus' friends. "Why are you looking up?" they asked. "Jesus has gone to Heaven. Someday He will come back to Earth the same way you saw Him leave."

> **You Can Pray:**
> Dear God, thank You for the Holy Spirit. He gives me power to tell others about Jesus. In Jesus' name. Amen.

Colton Currier   Age 7   Florida

Let's Talk:

1. How would the Holy Spirit help Jesus' friends?
2. What does it mean to witness?
3. What can you do when you are afraid to witness?

91. God Uses Peter

 Have you ever seen a miracle? A miracle is something only God can do. One man in the Bible really needed a miracle!

Jesus had returned to Heaven. One day His disciples, Peter and John, went to the temple. They saw a man who could not walk. Every day the man sat and begged. He saw Peter and John and asked them for money.

"I do not have money," Peter told the man. "I can give you what I have. In the name of Jesus, get up and walk!" Right away the man's legs were healed. It was a miracle! The man was so happy. He walked and jumped! He praised God!

God's Word Says:
"You are worthy, our Lord and God, to receive glory and honor [praise]. . . ."
Revelation 4:11

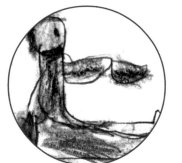 The people were amazed. "Why are you staring at us?" Peter asked. "We did not heal this man. Jesus did!" Peter praised God for what He had done.

You should praise God when He helps you do something well. Tell others how He helped you. Do not brag or act like you did it by yourself. Thank God for helping you. God is pleased when you thank Him for what He has done.

You Can Pray:
Dear God, thank You for all You do. Remind me to tell others how You have helped me. In Jesus' name. Amen.

Nathan Hane   Age 9   Missouri

Let's Talk:

1. What miracle did God do for the man who could not walk?
2. What did Peter tell the people after the man was healed?
3. What should you say when God helps you do something well?

92. Philip Obeys God

 Do you know God has a plan for your life? God knows what will happen every day. You can trust that His plan is best.

God had a plan for Philip, one of Jesus' disciples. Philip was teaching many people. An angel told him to go to the desert. Philip might not have understood but he obeyed.

> **God's Word Says:**
> "The LORD will guide you always. . . ."
> Isaiah 58:11

You may not understand something God wants you to do. Maybe your family has to move. God wants you to trust Him. He has a good plan for your life. God may have someone for you to help in that new place.

In the desert Philip saw a chariot—a big cart pulled by horses. The Holy Spirit said, "Go to that chariot." Philip obeyed.

A man in the chariot was reading God's Word. "Do you understand what you are reading?" Philip asked.

"I need someone to help me," the man said. Philip climbed in the chariot. He told the man it was Jesus he was reading about. The man believed in Jesus as his Savior!

Philip must have been glad he obeyed God's plan.

You Can Pray:
Dear God, You have a good plan for my life. Help me trust that Your plan is always best. In Jesus' name. Amen.

Chelsea Sihpol   Age 7   Colorado

Let's Talk:

1. Why did the angel tell Philip to go to the desert?

2. How did Philip help the man in the chariot?

3. Why should you follow God's plan for you?

93. Peter in Prison

Has anyone made fun of you because you believe in Jesus? Some people in the Bible were in real trouble because they were believers.

King Herod hated God's children. He even persecuted them. To persecute is to do mean things to someone because of what he or she believes. The king put many believers in prison.

One day the king put Peter in prison. Two soldiers were chained to Peter. Two others guarded the door. Peter knew he could be killed. He was not afraid. He trusted God and fell asleep. Peter's friends were praying for him.

That night God sent an angel. "Quick, get up!" the angel said. Peter's chains fell off. He followed the angel out the door. God had rescued him from prison!

God may choose to rescue you from a problem. Other times you may have to go through something hard. People may make fun of you or hurt you because you believe in Jesus.

God will use hard times to help you trust Him more. Keep being faithful to God. He will be with you no matter what happens.

You Can Pray:
Dear God, thank You for always being with me. I can trust You to take care of me no matter what! In Jesus' name. Amen.

This Bible story can be found in Acts 12:1-11.

Panov Petro   Age 9   Ukraine

Let's Talk:

1. How did God help Peter?
2. What does it mean to be persecuted?
3. How can God use hard times in your life?

94. Praying for Peter

Does God always answer prayer? He does not always say yes but God always answers. Peter's friends did not know that God had already answered their prayers!

An angel had rescued Peter from prison. Peter's friends had been at Mary's house praying for him. They heard a knock at the door. A girl named Rhoda went to see who it was. She heard Peter's voice. She was excited!

God's Word Says:
"Call to me and I will answer you. . . ."
Jeremiah 33:3

Rhoda did not open the door. She ran to tell the others. "You are crazy!" they said. They did not believe God had set Peter free. Finally they opened the door. There was Peter! God could have said no to their prayers. He could have said wait. Instead God said yes!

God will answer your prayers too. God is powerful enough to do anything. God is also wise. God may give you what you have prayed for right away. Other times you may have to wait for the answer to your prayer.

Sometimes God says no. He knows what you have asked for is not the best thing for you. Whatever answer God gives is best.

You Can Pray:
Dear God, thank You for your good answers to prayer. Help me remember Your answers are always best. In Jesus' name. Amen.

This Bible story can be found in Acts 12:11-17.

Lincoln Steconi Bispo dos Santos   Age 9   Brazil

Let's Talk:

1. How did God answer the prayers of Peter's friends?
2. What are some answers God may give to your prayers?
3. What is one prayer God has answered for you?

95. Saul's Conversion

Have you ever been sure you were right and found out you were wrong? A man named Saul was sure he was right.

Saul hated Christians—people who believed in Jesus. He did not believe that Jesus was God's Son. He wanted to stop Christians from telling people Jesus was alive again.

God's Word Says:
"Whoever believes in the Son has eternal life. . . ."
John 3:36

Saul took a trip to persecute Christians. Suddenly a bright light from Heaven shone on him. A voice said, "Saul, Saul, why do you persecute Me?"

Saul fell to the ground. He was afraid. "Who are You, Lord?" he asked.

"I am Jesus," the voice said. "I am the one you are persecuting." Saul was amazed. Jesus was really alive! He really is God's Son.

Do you believe Jesus is God's Son? He died and came alive again. You can believe He took the punishment for your sin. You can become a Christian.

The Bible says, "Whoever believes in the Son has eternal life . . ." (John 3:36). Believe in Jesus and trust Him to forgive your sins. Then you will have life that lasts forever with God in Heaven someday.

You Can Pray:
Dear God, thank You for Jesus, who died on the cross for me. Thank You that He came alive again. In Jesus' name. Amen.

Alek Rasouli   Age 10   Iran

Let's Talk:

1. Why was Saul persecuting Christians?
2. What did Saul learn about Jesus on his trip?
3. How can you become a Christian?

96. Ananias Visits Saul

Do you know God can use you to help other people? God wanted to use a Christian named Ananias.

Saul now believed in Jesus. When he got up from the ground, he could not see. His friends had to help him to the city. He spent the next three days praying.

God told Ananias to go find Saul and help him. Ananias did not want to go. He knew Saul persecuted Christians. He was afraid but God wanted him to help Saul.

God wants to use you to help others too! You need to be willing to obey. Maybe there is someone you do not like. God wants you to be kind and helpful to that person. You may be able to tell that person about Jesus.

Ananias did not want to obey. God said, "Go! I have chosen Saul to tell people about Jesus."

Ananias went and placed his hands on Saul. "Jesus sent me here so you may see again," he said. Right away Saul could see!

Ananias was glad he let God use him. Saul began telling people everywhere about Jesus!

You Can Pray:
Dear God, please use me to help others. Help me be willing to do what You want me to do. In Jesus' name. Amen.

This Bible story can be found in Acts 9:10-22.

Sara Boling Age 8 Indiana

Let's Talk:

1. How did God want to use Ananias?
2. Why was Ananias afraid to go and help Saul?
3. Who does God want you to help today?

97. Paul and Silas

? What do you do when something bad happens to you? What do you think God wants you to do? Read about Paul and Silas and find out!

In many places Saul was also known as Paul. He and his friend, Silas, taught people about Jesus. Sometimes this made people angry. One day Paul and Silas were beaten and put in jail. What did they do? They prayed and sang songs to God. They rejoiced! That is what God wants you to do.

> **God's Word Says:**
> "Rejoice in the Lord always. I will say it again: Rejoice!"
> Philippians 4:4

To rejoice means to be joyful and praise God. Even if you are sad or angry, you can still thank God. He loves and cares for you. He will work things out in the best way. You can even sing your praise to God!

When Paul and Silas rejoiced, the other prisoners heard them. Then an earthquake shook the prison! The doors came open and their chains fell off.

The jailer was afraid. He thought he was in big trouble. Paul and Silas told him no one had escaped. They told the jailer about Jesus. He believed and so did his family!

You Can Pray:
Dear God, thank You for taking care of me. Please help me rejoice even when things are hard. In Jesus' name. Amen.

Edmond Fyeidale   Age 10   Zimbabwe

Let's Talk:

1. What does it mean to rejoice?
2. How did Paul and Silas rejoice in prison?
3. How can you rejoice when something bad happens?

98. Paul's Shipwreck

 Do you ever feel like giving up? Some men on a ship with Paul may have felt like giving up.

Paul had been beaten and put in jail many times for telling people about Jesus. Now he was a prisoner again. He was on a ship going to the city of Rome.

 A terrible storm began. Big waves splashed into the ship. The men with Paul were afraid the ship would sink! The storm lasted for 14 days!

Paul was not afraid. God had promised that Paul would tell people in Rome about Jesus. God had also promised that everyone on the ship would be safe. Paul did not give up. He trusted God's promises.

Do you sometimes feel like giving up? Maybe there is something at school that is hard for you. Maybe you think you will never be good at anything. Do not give up! Trust God's promise to help you.

Paul was trusting God. He prayed. God told him how to keep everyone safe. God kept His promise. The ship broke apart but everyone made it safely to shore.

 You Can Pray:
Dear God, thank You for Your promises. Help me trust You and not give up. In Jesus' name. Amen.

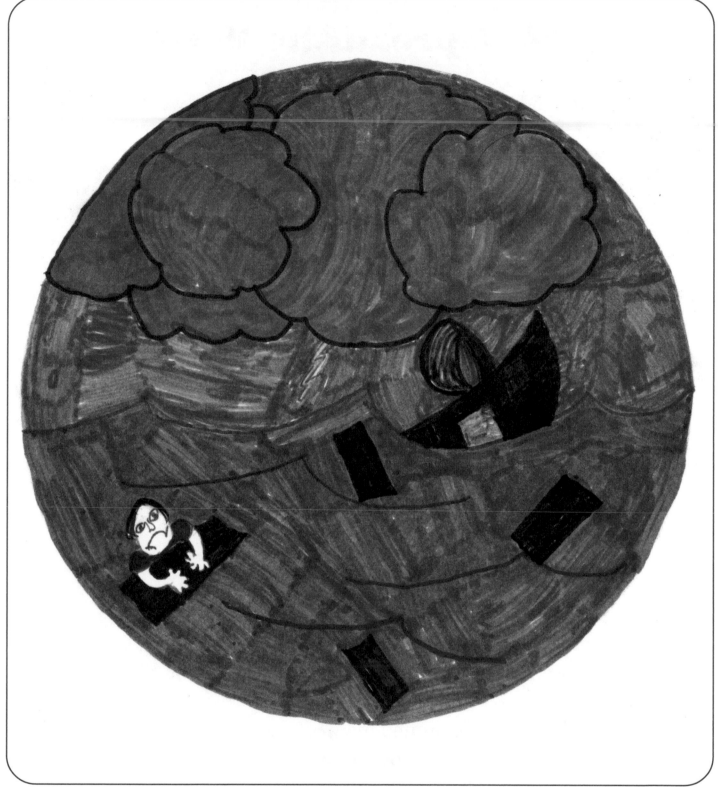

Breahann Martin   Age 10   West Virginia

Let's Talk:

1. Why were the men on the ship afraid?
2. What kept Paul from giving up?
3. What should you do when you feel like giving up?

99. Spread the Word

What job did Jesus give His disciples before He went back to Heaven? He wanted them to tell others about Him!

Jesus said, "Go into all the world and preach the good news." Paul and other Christians told people about Jesus in many parts of the world.

Some people today still have never heard about Jesus. They need to know that He can save them from sin. Are you telling others about Jesus? You can witness anywhere you are. God wants every Christian to be a witness.

God has chosen some people to be missionaries. Their work in life is to help others know about Jesus. Some missionaries are teachers or doctors. Others may be builders or pilots.

Some missionaries work in their own countries. Others go to another country. They tell people about Jesus. Someday God may ask you to be a missionary. Are you willing to obey Him?

Telling people around the world about Jesus is a big job. You do not have to do it alone! Jesus said, "I am with you always." He will help you.

You Can Pray:
Dear God, I want to be a witness for You. Make me willing to do whatever You want me to do with my life. In Jesus' name. Amen.

Seth Johns   Age 5   Missouri

Let's Talk:

1. What job did Jesus give to believers?
2. What is a missionary?
3. What does God want you to be willing to do?

100. Be Ready!

 Have you ever gone on a trip? How do you get ready? Someday God's children will go on a much bigger trip—to Heaven!

Jesus promised to come back again. All those who have believed in Jesus will rise up to meet Him in the air. They will live with God in Heaven forever.

God's Word Says:
"So you also must be ready, because the Son of Man [Jesus] will come. . . ."
Matthew 24:44

 Heaven will be much better than Earth. No one will sin. No one will die. No one will cry or get hurt. Everyone will always be happy!

How can you be ready for Heaven? You need to know Jesus as your Savior. If you do know Him, you will want to obey His Word.

Read your Bible and do what it says. If you do not have a Bible, you can learn the Bible verses in this book. Talk to God in prayer each day. God wants His children to become more like Jesus.

No one knows when Jesus will come back. That will be the best day ever! For the first time you will see God. Be sure you are ready to meet Him!

 You Can Pray:
Dear God, thank You that I am ready for Heaven. I have believed in Jesus. Help me read Your Word and talk to You each day. In Jesus' name. Amen.

This Bible story can be found in
1 Thessalonians 4:16-18; Revelation 21:1-5; 22:11-12.

Allison Fieger   Age 9   Pennsylvania

Let's Talk:

1. What will happen to believers when Jesus comes back?
2. What does a person need to do to be ready for Heaven?
3. What can believers do to become more like Jesus?

Index of Stories

Old Testament Stories

New Testament Stories

Subject Index

This is a list of some of the subjects in this book.
The numbers show which page to look at to read about that subject.

Project Coordinator: Lynda E. Pongracz

General Editors: Lynda E. Pongracz and Brenda J. Hanson

Text Editors: Cynthia H. Channell, Yolanda Derstine and Deborah Koenig

Development Team: Ron Hane, Brenda J. Hanson, Jerry W. Hanson, Wanda Hearing, Michael J. Neigh, Lora Oates, Marshall J. Pennell, Lynda E. Pongracz and Leah Pruitt

Writers: Lisa J. Deam, Brenda J. Hanson, Lora Oates and Lynda E. Pongracz

Theological Consultants: Rev. William Cox, Rev. Jerry Hanson, Rev. Phil McCoy, Dr. Timothy D. Martin, Rev. Jim Neigh, Marshall J. Pennell, Rev. Richard Rhea and Rev. Brian Thom

Educational Consultants: Julie Cox, Cheryl Oetting and Leah Pruitt

Graphic Design: Kaori Armstrong

Illustrations: The pictures throughout this book are original drawings created by children from 23 countries and 15 states and used by permission. We appreciate each child's part in making this book colorful and fun. Thanks to all the people who collected and made the children's drawings available for this project.

Cover: Designed by Stephen R. Bates

The Wonder Early Reader Devotional Book: Helping Kids Get the Big Picture

ISBN 1-55976-575-5

Printed in the United States of America

Do you like to get mail?

You can join the *CEF Mailbox Club*™! You will get free Bible lessons in the mail.

After you do the lesson you can send it back to us. Your *CEF Mailbox Club* friend will check your lesson. Then you will get a new lesson in the mail.

You have already learned a lot about God in this book. Now you can learn even more about Him!

Are you ready to join the *CEF Mailbox Club?* Ask your mom or dad to fill out the coupon below. Cut it out and put it in an envelope. Add a stamp and mail it to:

> CEF Mailbox Club
> PO Box 190
> Warrenton, MO 63383-0190

Name _____ Birthday _____ Age _____ Grade _____

Parent/Guardian _____

Mailing Address _____ Apt. # _____

City _____ State _____ Zip _____